EGO PSYCHOLOGY AND THE
PROBLEM OF ADAPTATION

Journal of the American Psychoanalytic Association
Monograph Series Number One

EGO PSYCHOLOGY AND THE PROBLEM OF ADAPTATION

HEINZ HARTMANN

Translated by DAVID RAPAPORT

INTERNATIONAL UNIVERSITIES PRESS, INC.
Madison   Connecticut

Copyright 1958, by Heinz Hartmann, M.D.
Library of Congress Catalog Card Number: 58-13783

Fourteenth Printing, 1995

Manufactured in the United States of America

Contents

Preface	vii
Author's Note	xi
1. The Conflict-Free Ego Sphere	3
2. Adaptation	22
3. Adaptation and "Fitting Together"—The Reality Principle	38
4. Ego Development and Adaptation	48
5. Internalization, Thinking, and Rational Behavior	57
6. Some Integrative Functions of the Ego	74
7. Implications for the Concepts of Health and Education	80
8. Preconscious Automatisms	86
9. Ego Apparatuses. Autonomous Ego Development	100
Bibliography	109
Name Index	115
Subject Index	117

Preface

THE publication of a complete English translation of Heinz Hartmann's essay, EGO PSYCHOLOGY AND THE PROBLEM OF ADAPTATION, inaugurates the Monograph Series of the Journal of the American Psychoanalytic Association. This project was conceived several years ago, but its initiation has had to await the availability of a psychoanalytic work of exceptional merit and importance. The editors believe that the appropriate occasion has finally arrived. The timeliness of this decision is attested to by the recent award to Dr. Hartmann, of the Charles Frederick Menninger Award of the American Psychoanalytic Association, for his scientific contributions.

"Ich-Psychologie und Anpassungsproblem" was first presented in 1937 before the Vienna Psychoanalytic Society and then published in German in 1939 in the *Internationale Zeitschrift für Psychoanalyse und Imago*. Historically it represents a turning point in the development of modern psychoanalytic theory. It is a natural sequel to Freud's previous formulations of the structural hypothesis and his contributions to ego psychology. With its appearance there began an evolution in psychoanalytic thought which continues to

PREFACE

ramify and the full implications of which for theory and practice are not yet fully realized.

To readers intimately acquainted with current psychoanalytic ego psychology, this essay will reveal the first formulations of some of its basic concepts. Many of them will have a ring of familiarity, because of the remarkable degree to which Hartmann's ideas have shaped, and become assimilated into, current psychoanalytic thinking. One becomes aware of the tremendous impact of his theories when one finds that it was in this essay that concepts such as the undifferentiated phase, the conflict-free ego sphere, conflict-free ego development, and primary and secondary autonomy were developed for the first time. Hartmann discusses the role of endowment and of the inborn ego apparatuses and their adaptive nature. The idea that ego defenses may simultaneously serve the control of instinctual drives and the adaptation to the external world finds its expression in this essay. Hartmann's concept of adaptation is in no way restricted to the "cultural" sense of the term. It is a truly inclusive conception, and he views it as an ongoing process, which has its roots in the biological structure, and with many of its manifestations reflecting the constant attempts of the ego to balance intrasystemic and intersystemic tensions. The implications of his theory for the development of perception and thought processes, the concepts of ego strength, ego weakness, and of normality, are also discussed. Neutralization, and the impact of this construct on the concept of sublimation, evolves quite naturally from this paper.

One sees in this work a systematic attempt to establish within the framework of a psychoanalytic ego psychology the groundwork for a theory of human behavior in general, normal as well as abnormal. The great sweep of Hartmann's exceptionally rich intellect has made it possible for him in

PREFACE

this task to integrate the whole field of psychoanalytic knowledge with the related fields of biology, psychology, sociology, and philosophy.

The opportunity to read this essay will reintroduce psychoanalysts to a cardinal requirement of the scientific method which Dr. Hartmann's work demonstrates, namely his unswerving insistence upon precision in methodology, and upon logical consistency of theory. With it all, the rarified atmosphere of theory is flavored by a humanistic tolerance and understanding, which is discernible in his discussions of rational and irrational behavior, automatism and mechanisms of integration.

The fact that this paper has never before been published in its entirety in English left a void in the psychoanalytic literature for English-reading psychoanalysts. This is now being filled by the decision of the Journal of the American Psychoanalytic Association to publish this essay as its first Monograph. We are proud to make it available to the many students of psychoanalysis who have never known the full content of this classic essay.

The efforts of many were required to carry out this project. Foremost among these is Dr. David Rapaport, who originally translated and published excerpts of this work in his book, *Organization and Pathology of Thought,* but who for the purposes of this Monograph prepared a completely new translation. His great familiarity with the work in its original form, as well as the fact that Dr. Hartmann himself has participated in the elucidation of certain crucial points, provides assurance of the authoritative stature of this English version of the original German article. In addition to our great indebtedness to Dr. Rapaport, we wish to express our gratitude to the Ford Foundation, whose grant-in-aid to the

PREFACE

Austen Riggs Center permitted Dr. Rapaport and his associates to carry out the preparation of the translation.

We also wish to thank Dr. Merton Gill for his assistance with the primary translation; Miss Suzette H. Annin who is actually the co-translator and fully responsible for the English of this Monograph; and Miss Rosemary Ranzoni who was responsible for the typing of the many versions of this translation. Finally, we acknowledge with great appreciation the over-all editorial assistance, as well as bibliographical work, of Mrs. Lottie Maury Newman, Editor of International Universities Press. It is this combined effort which we hope will make the publication of this first of the Monograph Series of the Journal of the American Psychoanalytic Association a noteworthy event.

THE EDITORS

Author's Note

THIS ESSAY, which appeared in German some twenty years ago, is published here essentially unchanged. I still consider most of the thoughts presented in it to be valid. Some of them were developed further, reformulated, or were stated more systematically in subsequent papers. Nonetheless, I feel that a close study of historical developments in psychoanalysis is still one main prerequisite for its fuller understanding. I decided therefore to have this essay published in its original form rather than to rewrite it in conformity with the present state of our knowledge. Footnotes added in this edition (indicated by brackets) will guide the reader to subsequent developments in my work of the subjects dealt with in this paper.

I wish to express my warmest gratitude to Dr. David Rapaport. I am fully aware how much resourcefulness and scholarly labor went into this revised translation of the complete essay.

HEINZ HARTMANN

March, 1958
New York

EGO PSYCHOLOGY AND THE
PROBLEM OF ADAPTATION

1.

The Conflict-Free Ego Sphere

PSYCHOANALYSIS encounters the issue of adaptation in three forms: as a problem of its ego psychology, as a therapeutic aim, and as an educational consideration. It is striking that while the concept "ego syntonic" is fairly well defined, experience shows that the term "reality syntonic" is so elastic that it covers diverse and even partly contradictory views.

Psychoanalysis alone cannot solve the problem of adaptation. It is a subject of research for biology and sociology also. However, the important insights psychoanalysis has given, and will give, into adaptation could hardly be attained by the other approaches and methods. Therefore we have the right to expect that all investigations of the problem of adaptation take into account the fundamental facts and relationships discovered by psychoanalysis. The increase of our interest in the problems of adaptation is due mainly to those developments in psychoanalysis which focused our attention on ego functions; but it was also fostered by our increased interest in the total personality, as well as by the concern over certain theoretical formulations about mental health, which use "adjustment to reality" as a criterion.

I shall have to touch on some matters which are well known, on some which may be controversial, and on a few which are not, strictly speaking, psychoanalytic. But all that

I have to say is, I believe, in accord with the basic views of psychoanalysis. I maintain that it is a psychoanalytic endeavor—in the broader sense—to transfer concepts which were developed in reference to concrete problems of the personality's central sphere to other realms of mental life, and to study the changes in these concepts necessitated by the conditions prevailing in these other realms.

I shall begin with a few comments on the scope of the problem within the limits I have set for myself, without attempting to give a systematic statement of it.

Psychoanalysis evinced quite early, and perhaps even from the very beginning, a narrower and a broader objective. It started out with the study of pathology and of phenomena which are on the border of normal psychology and psychopathology. At that time its work centered on the id and the instinctual drives. But soon there arose new problems, concepts, formulations, and new needs for explanation, which reached beyond this narrower field toward a *general* theory of mental life. A decisive, and perhaps the most clearly delineated, step in this direction is our recent ego psychology: Freud's work of the last fifteen years; and then—following the pathways of investigation which he opened—primarily Anna Freud's studies, and, in another area, those of the English school. At present we no longer doubt that psychoanalysis can claim to be a *general* psychology in the broadest sense of the word, and our conception of the working methods which may properly be considered psychoanalytic has become broader, deeper, and more discriminating.

Anna Freud (1936, pp. 4-5) defined the goal of psychoanalysis as the attainment of the fullest possible knowledge of the three mental institutions. But not every effort in psychology which contributes to this goal can be considered psychoanalytic. The distinctive characteristic of a psychoanalytic investigation is not its subject matter but the scientific methodology, and the structure of the concepts it uses. All psychological investigations share some of their objectives with psychoanalysis. These partially shared goals bring into particularly sharp relief the distinctive characteristics of psychoanalytic thinking. (Consider, for instance, the contrast between psychoanalytic ego psychology and Alfred Adler's psychology.) Recent developments in psychoanalysis have not changed its salient characteristics, namely its biological orientation, its genetic, dynamic, economic, and topographic points of view, and the explanatory nature of its concepts. Thus, when psychoanalysis and nonanalytic psychology study the same subject matter, they will, of necessity, arrive at different results. In the last analysis, they differ in their view of what is essential, and this inevitably leads them to different descriptive and relational propositions. A similar situation exists in anatomy, where descriptively insignificant characteristics may be ontogenetically or phylogenetically crucial; and in chemistry, where coal and diamond are identical analytically, though from other points of view they are strikingly different. In general, characteristics which are relevant in a broader theory may be irrelevant in a more limited context. Though these are merely analogies, they do make a valid point, since psychoanalysis does have the potentiality to become a general theory of mental development, broader, both in its assumptions and scope, than any other psychological theory. To realize this potentiality, however, we must survey from the point of view of psychoanalysis, and encompass within our theory, those psychological phenomena which were the subject matter of psychology before psychoanalysis existed, as well as those which are now the subject matter of psychology, but not of psychoanalysis.

It has often been said that while the psychology of the id

was and remains a "preserve" of psychoanalysis, ego psychology is its general meeting ground with nonanalytic psychology. Even the objections against psychoanalytic ego psychology differ from those leveled against id psychology; they are like those commonly encountered in scientific criticism—less hostile and less categorical. To some psychoanalysts this is evidence that the findings of ego psychology are invalid or unimportant. But this is unjustified: the resistance to a new discovery is clearly not a direct measure of its scientific significance. It is also conceivable that ego psychology is criticized more mildly only because nonanalysts rarely grasp its background and implications. Even though Freud rightly declined to regard psychoanalysis as a "system," it is nevertheless a cohesive organization of propositions, and any attempt to isolate parts of it not only destroys its over-all unity, but also changes and invalidates its parts. Consequently, psychoanalytic ego psychology differs radically from the "surface psychologies," even though—as Fenichel (1937b) has pointed out recently—it is, and will be, increasingly interested in the details of behavior, in all the shadings of conscious experience, in the rarely studied preconscious processes, and in the relationships between the unconscious, preconscious, and conscious ego. The dynamic and economic points of view, though they apply to all mental life, have been scarcely applied to these. The history of the development of psychoanalytic psychology explains why we understand as yet relatively little about those processes and working methods of the mental apparatus which lead to *adapted achievements*. We cannot simply contrast the ego as the nonbiological part of the personality with the id as its biological part; the very problem of adaptation warns against such a division, but about this more will have to be said later on. It is, however, true and also natural that pure phenomenological description of the details of the mental superficies, which we could disregard previously, is essential for and attains a special importance in ego psychology. But we will probably all agree that these phenomenological details, which nowadays command our interest, serve us merely as points of departure. The goal of gathering a maximum of descriptive detail is indeed the goal of phenomenological psychology, but not of psychoanalytic ego psychology: there lies the fundamental difference between the two. For instance, Federn's ego psychology, which focuses on varieties of ego experiences, is certainly not just a phenomenology: the varieties of experience serve it as indicators of other (libidinal) processes and are treated in terms of explanatory rather than descriptive concepts.

The close connection between theory and therapeutic technique, so characteristic of psychoanalysis, explains why the ego functions directly involved in the *conflicts* between the mental institutions commanded our interest earlier than others. It also explains why other ego functions and the process of coming to terms with the environment—except for a few pertinent problems which played a role in psychoanalysis from the beginning—did not become the subject matter of research until a later stage of our science. Psychoanalytic observation has frequently come upon facts and considerations related to these other ego functions, but rarely subjected them to detailed study and theoretical reflection. I believe it is an empirical fact that these functions are less decisive for the understanding and treatment of pathology—on which psychoanalytic interest has been centered so far—than the psychology of the conflicts which are at the root of every neurosis. I am not inclined, however, to underestimate the clinical importance of these functions, though here I shall deal mainly with their theoretical significance, and even with that from only a single point of view. We must recognize that though the ego certainly does grow on conflicts, these are not the only roots of ego development. Many of us expect psychoanalysis to become a general *developmental psychology:* to do so, it must encompass these other roots of ego development, by reanalyzing from its own point of view and with its own methods the results obtained in these areas by nonanalytic psychology. This naturally gives new importance to the direct observation of developmental processes by psychoanalysts (first of all the direct observation of children).

Not every adaptation to the environment, or every learning and maturation process, is a conflict. I refer to the development *outside of conflict* of perception, intention, object comprehension, thinking, language, recall-phenomena, productivity, to the well-known phases of motor development, grasping, crawling, walking, and to the maturation and learning processes implicit in all these and many others. Many well-known psychoanalytic studies, which I will not list here, have taken these for their point of departure. Naturally, most of them do not treat these problems from the point of view of present-day ego psychology. (The vicissitudes of psychoanalytic drive psychology and ego psychology were surveyed by E. Bibring, 1936.) I need not list here all these functions: you know them. I certainly do not imply that the childhood activities I have enumerated, and other relevant ones as well, remain untouched by mental conflict; nor do I imply that disturbances in their development do not in turn give rise to conflicts, nor that they do not get embroiled in other conflicts. On the contrary, I want to stress that their vicissitudes play an important role in the well-known typical and individual developments and conflicts of instinctual drives, and in facilitating or hampering the individual's ability to master these. I propose that we adopt the provisional term *conflict-free ego sphere* for that ensemble of functions which at any given time exert their effects outside the region of mental conflicts. I do not want to be misunderstood: I am not speaking of a province of the mind, the development of which is in principle immune to conflicts, but rather of processes *in so far as,* in an individual, they remain empirically outside of the sphere of mental conflict. It is quite possible to state, both for the cross-sectional and the longitudinal aspects of an individual's mental life, what belongs to this conflict-free sphere. What we do not yet have is a systematic psychoanalytic knowledge of this sphere; we have only partial knowledge of reality-fears, of defense processes in so far as they result in "normal" development, of the conflict-free sphere's contributions to the kinds and consequences of defense (and resistance), its contributions to the displacement of the aims of instinctual drives, and so on. We do not need to prove that investigations which are *limited* to this sphere, as those of academic psychology usually are, inevitably overlook basic psychological relationships.

It is probable that the study of this conflict-free ego sphere, though it is certainly not without technical significance (for instance, in the analysis of resistance), will in general contribute less to psychoanalytic technique than the study of conflicts and defenses; this problem, however, will not concern us here. It might be argued that this sphere includes just that part of mental happening which must remain beyond the scope of psychoanalytic endeavor, and is better left to other psychological disciplines. I have already indicated why such a limitation and resignation are unjustified. Psychology cannot be divided between psychoanalysis and other psychological disciplines, because the latter overlook developmental facts which are crucial even in those areas customarily considered "extra-analytic." If we take seriously the claim of psychoanalysis to be a general theory of mental development, we must study this area of psychology too, from our points of view and with our methods, both by analysis and by direct observation of infant development. The conflict-free ego sphere is now, as all of ego psychology used to be, "that other realm" which, though it had to be entered at every turn, could not be theoretically accounted for. But this limitation, too, will soon disappear.

Adaptation obviously involves both processes connected with conflict situations, and processes which pertain to the conflict-free sphere. It was in connection with the problem of adaptation that I first encountered the issues discussed here. It would be, for instance, an enticing task to trace, in a concrete case, the interaction of those processes which assimilate the external and the internal stimuli and lead to average adaptiveness and normal adaptation, with those mechanisms which we know better and consider to be causes of developmental disturbances. It would be equally interesting to trace such interactions in many problems of character development, in that aspect of the personality which we call "ego interests," and so forth. For instance, the influence of special talents on the distribution of narcissistic, object-libidinal and aggressive energies, their role in facilitating certain forms of conflict solution and in determining the choice of preferred defenses, are clinically important but insufficiently studied problems. Hermann (1923) made a significant contribution to the psychoanalytic study of special talents, but from a different point of view. The concrete study of various ego disturbances in psychoses and of some of the psychophysical interrelations must also take into account this conflict-free sphere. None of these problems can be completely resolved in terms of instinctual drives and conflicts.

Our knowledge of the ego began with its defense functions, as Anna Freud's (1936) classic study shows. However, there are problems—and I must stress that these arose in the field

THE CONFLICT-FREE EGO SPHERE

of psychoanalysis—which make it necessary for us to study other ego functions and other aspects of ego activity also. The development of the ego may be described by tracing those conflicts which it must solve in its struggle with the id and the superego, and if we include the conflicts with the external world also, then we see it in terms of the war it wages on three fronts. But, to use an analogy, the description of a country, a nation, a state, includes, besides its involvements in wars with neighboring nations or states, its boundaries and the peacetime traffic across the borders. (This is only one of the possible analogies: for instance what is here the borderland forms an essential part of what we call, in our more usual analogy, the "central region" of the personality.) It also includes the peaceful development of its populace, economy, social structure, administration, etc. A state may also be regarded as a system of institutions, which function through legislation, jurisdiction, etc. Obviously, there are systematic relationships between these various points of view, and, returning to our psychological point of departure, these relationships will interest us the most. Our task is to investigate how mental conflict and "peaceful" internal development mutually facilitate and hamper each other. We must, likewise, study the interplay between conflict and that aspect of development with which we are familiar mostly from its relations to the external world. Thus, to take a simple example, learning to walk upright combines constitution, maturation of the apparatus, and learning processes, with those libidinal processes, identifications, endogenous and exogenous (instinctual drive and environmental) factors which may lead to conflicts and to disturbances of function (cf. M. Schmideberg, 1937). None of these processes alone can explain this important step in development.

It would be an error, however, to assume that the contrast

of conflict situation and peaceful development corresponds directly to the antithesis of pathological and normal. The normal human being is free neither of problems nor of conflicts. Conflicts are part of the human condition. Naturally, conflicts have a different range and intensity in pathological than in normal cases. The antitheses, pathological versus normal, defense-born versus not-defense-born (or: development resulting from conflict versus conflict-free development) do not coincide: the former contrasts disturbance with achievement, the latter contrasts conflict with the absence of conflict. A "successful" defense may amount to a "failure" in achievement and vice versa. An explicit restatement of this commonplace may not be superfluous, since experience shows that quite often no distinction is made between these two antitheses. By stating this I do not mean to question that (for obvious reasons) the most fruitful approach to the problem of conflict was the study of disturbed function and that it is still uncertain whether the exploration of the conflict-free sphere will use primarily the same approach, or rather that of the (direct and indirect) observation of undisturbed development.

Of the fields studied or influenced by psychoanalysis, education and sociology, for instance, stand to gain by our broadening our horizon in the direction of the conflict-free sphere and adaptation. It is easy to show where the points of departure for such broadening are in ego psychology, by reexamining a few familiar problems from a new angle. Since Anna Freud's work contains the first exhaustive statement of an important group of ego functions, I will choose my examples from her work. These examples will stress only a point of view and will not bring anything new to psychoanalysis. In the historical part of the paper she gave at the Congress in Budapest, Anna Freud (1937) demonstrated that the vicissitudes of psychoanalytic theory and the changing focus of psychoanalytic interest are reflected in the psychoanalytic view of education: each extension of theoretical awareness results in the recognition and correction of lopsided views in education. There was a time, for instance, when "the prevention of neurosis" was considered to be the heart of the psychoanalytic contribution to education. Indeed, at that time, both written and oral communications seemed to convey the expectation that not only education but the entire history of culture would become simply part of "the prevention of neurosis." Anna Freud has also shown that a more precise psychoanalytic understanding of the ego must change education, both in its general direction and in its handling of the individual case. I think it is permissible to continue this train of thought in the light of what I have just said. So far, psychoanalytic ego psychology has been predominantly a conflict psychology; the conflict-free avenues of a reality-adapted development have remained peripheral to it. A science is entitled to feel its way from one result to the next; empirical sciences must do so. Education, however, is always built on a —scientific or unscientific—conception of the total personality, and its goals are social norms which specifically pertain to adaptive achievements (the one exception to this we will discuss later). Therefore, an educational approach has a social chance (for the moment we disregard the implied problem of values) only if it takes into account all facets of development, their structure, their biological rank order, and their value for achievement and adaptation.

For instance, some of the relationships between the instinctual drives and *mental development* are well known. We know how conflicts and taboos involving instinctual drives may hamper intellectual development, temporarily or permanently. On the other hand, Anna Freud has shown that intellectualization may serve as a defense against instinctual danger in puberty, representing an attempt to master the instinctual drive by indirect means. But this process has another, reality-oriented, aspect also, showing that this mechanism of defense against instinctual drives may at the same time be regarded as an adaptation process. It is in this sense that Anna Freud (1936, p. 179) says: "instinctual danger makes human beings intelligent." We are entitled to ask: what determines the choice of just this means of instinctual drive mastery? and what determines the extent of intellectualization a person will use? We are familiar with part of these certainly complex interrelationships: for example, with the developmental significance of early infantile attempts at solutions. We may, however, safely assume an autonomous intelligence factor which, as an independent variable, codetermines the choice and success of the defensive process. Though we are not completely ignorant about these matters, we do not have a systematic knowledge of them. Learning to think and learning in general are independent biological functions which exist alongside, and in part independent of, instinctual drives and defenses.

Ordered thinking is always directly or indirectly reality-oriented. When a defense against instinctual drives results in heightened intellectual achievements, this shows that certain forms of conflict solution may involve biological guarantees of an adaptation process to external reality. This does not hold for all defense processes, of course, but it does hold for intellectualization even outside of pubertal development. "This intellectualization of instinctual life, the attempt to lay hold on the instinctual processes by connecting them with ideas which can be dealt with in consciousness, is one of the most general, earliest and most necessary acquirements of the human ego. We regard it not as an activity of the ego, but

THE CONFLICT-FREE EGO SPHERE

as one of its indispensable components" (Anna Freud, 1936, p. 178).

Thus the description of this phenomenon as a defense does not fully define it. The definition must also include its reality-oriented and adaptation-facilitating characteristics and regulations. More generally, we are interested in what manner and to what extent is defense indirectly regulated by those ego functions which are not currently involved in the conflict. After all, mental development is not simply the outcome of the struggle with instinctual drives, with love-objects, with the superego, and so on. For instance, we have reason to assume that this development is served by apparatuses which function from the beginning of life; but about this, more later on. For now, we will mention only that memory, associations, and so on, are functions which cannot possibly be derived from the ego's relationships to instinctual drives or love-objects, but are rather *prerequisites* of our conception of these and of their development.

In judging the success of a defense we will inquire not only into the fate of the instinctual drive and the protection afforded to the ego, but also—more than before—into its effects on the ego functions not directly involved in the conflict. The concepts of ego strength, ego weakness, ego restriction, etc., are all related to this realm, but they remain nebulous as long as the specific ego functions involved are not studied in detail. Ego strength—though it manifests itself strikingly in the struggles of the conflict-sphere—cannot be defined solely in terms of that borderland of the ego which is involved in the conflict. In terms of our analogy, the effectiveness of the armies defending the borders also depends on the support they get or do not get from the rear. Once we have determined objectively those factors of ability, character, will, etc., which are the empirical—not theoretical—correlates of "strong" or "weak" egos, we will have escaped the relativity of the usual definitions which determine ego strength from the individual ego's relation to its id or superego. We will then be able to compare the ego strength of different individuals, even though the relationship between mastery of reality and achievement on the one hand, and ego strength on the other, is very complex. Hendrick's (1936) study is a step toward such a definition of ego strength.

In our clinical work we observe daily how differences in intellectual development, in motor development, and so on, affect the child's coping with conflicts and how this in turn influences intellectual and motor development. Such observations establish descriptively the interaction of the conflict-sphere with other ego functions. This is an *actual interaction*—that is to say, this too is an instance of the overdetermination of a mental process. Yet, depending on the manner in which we encounter these phenomena, we may also speak about two *aspects* of the ego process, since, for instance, it is often one and the same process which we study first in its relation to the internal conflict and then in its dependence and effect on the apparatuses of reality mastery. At one point we may be interested in the pathology of a process, in its genetic relationship to adaptation disturbances, and at another point, in the positive adaptation value it gains in another context. Our vantage point determines which aspect of the process will assume importance: the two relationships pertain to two different points of view (cf. pp. 80ff. on health and conflict).

For another example I will choose *fantasy*, and it will lead us to the same conclusion. It, too, is important in child psychology and education, but we also deal with it continuously in the analysis of adults. I need not remind you of the role of fantasy formation, in the strict sense of the word, in the psychology of neuroses. In her recent volume, Anna Freud

(1936) discusses the function of fantasy in the development of the child. She examines the denial of reality in fantasy and shows how the child, refusing to accept a disagreeable bit of reality, can, under certain conditions, deny its existence and replace it by fantasy formations. This is a process within the limits of normal ego development. Anna Freud asks what determines whether or not such a process becomes pathological. Presumably, this depends on a number of factors. Among these, the degree of maturity of those ego apparatuses of perception, thinking, and particularly causal thinking, and so on, which guarantee the relationship of the human being to his environment, certainly plays an outstanding role. Anna Freud wrote: "... perhaps ... the attachment of the mature ego to reality is in general stronger than that of the infantile ego ..." (1936, p. 87). From the point of view of mental economy it is a very different matter when a fantasy replaces an important piece of reality in the adult, than when this occurs in the child. Here again, as in the development and inhibition of intelligence, we must study the function and development of the ego apparatuses we have referred to, because without knowledge about these our question cannot be answered. (Psychological investigations have reached some pertinent results: they have established a relationship between fantasy and eidetic endowment, the latter of which, according to Jaensch [1923], "implies potentialities both for significant achievements and for a dreamy fantastic existence." Which of these courses will be taken is, however, determined by the total personality and not by the eidetic endowment. Thus, in regard to the crucial question, academic psychology again leaves us in the lurch.)

Continuing our preceding considerations, we must now ask: what are the positive adaptive elements of fantasy? In answering this question, we will certainly not forget the basic biological significance of reality testing, particularly the distinction between fantasy and reality. Varendonck (1921), the only psychoanalytic author after Freud to investigate the general characteristics of fantasy thinking, maintained that the biological significance of fantasy thinking, in contrast to dream work, lies in its attempts to solve problems of waking life. As an aside I want to mention that in Varendonck's study of fantasy we again encounter those preconscious mechanisms whose significance for our problem was recently stressed also by Kris (1939). Fantasy is a broad and somewhat vague concept. Yet all the phenomena so labeled are apparently in some degree related to each other. It is general knowledge that fantasy—not just in the sense of a talent for making new combinations, but also in the sense of symbolic, pictorial thought—can be fruitful even in scientific thinking, supposedly the undisputed domain of rational thought. A rigid view of mental health to the contrary notwithstanding, the healthy adult's mental life is probably never quite free of the denial and replacement of some reality by fantasy formation. Religious ideas and attitudes toward infantile sexuality are examples.

It is possible, and even probable, that the relationship to reality is learned by way of *detours*. There are avenues of reality-adaptation which, at first, certainly lead away from the real situation. The function of play is a good example, that is, its actual role in human development rather than any teleological theories about it. Another example is the auxiliary function of fantasy in the learning process: though fantasy always implies an initial turning away from a real situation, it can also be a preparation for reality and may lead to a better mastery of it. Fantasy may fulfill a synthetic function by provisionally connecting our needs and goals with possible ways of realizing them. It is well known that there are fantasies which, while they remove man from external reality, open up for him his internal reality. The basic facts of mental life were the contents of such "fantasies" long before psychoanalysis made them amenable to scientific investigation. The primary function of these fantasies is autoplastic rather than alloplastic; but we should be the last to deny the general importance of increased insight into intrapsychic life, and its particular importance in the mastery of the external world.

I must point out that *knowledge of reality* is not synonymous with *adaptation to reality*. But more about this later on. This, too, is an example of the already mentioned necessity to separate the different aspects of adaptation. The situation appears paradoxical: taking our point of departure from pathology, from the psychology of neuroses and psychoses, we come to overestimate the positive developmental significance of the shortest pathways to reality, and it is only when we set out from the problem of reality-adaptation that we recognize the positive value of the detour through fantasy. Yet, actually, it is the same phenomenon which, considered first from one and then from the other point of view, attains positive or negative emphasis. From the first point of view "positive" means "neurosis prevention"; from the second, it means "general furtherance of adaptation." Only a premature and one-sided evaluation could disregard this essential unity. For a long time psychoanalysis had no occasion to deal with that other aspect of these processes which belongs to the realm of normal psychology, but is, naturally, not understood by non-psychoanalytic normal psychology.

Denial is based on flight, and *avoidance* even more clearly so. Anna Freud (1936) has shown us how they both result in ego restriction. But avoidance of the environment in which difficulties are encountered—and its positive correlate, the search for one which offers easier and better possibilities for action—is also a most effective adaptation process (which, by the way, transcends the common antithesis of autoplastic and alloplastic adaptations). The search for a favorable environment among those available (and likewise for the most favorable of the possible functions) should probably be given a far more central position among adaptation processes—in the broader sense—than is customary (cf. A. E. Parr, 1926). In the animal kingdom it is easy to trace this process, and no doubt there are countless examples of it in human behavior also. So denial and avoidance too involve that other group of ego tendencies.

What holds—in this regard—for fantasies also holds for *affective action*. From the point of view of the psychology of neuroses, affective action—in contrast to the theoretical ideal of rational action—often appears as a deplorable residue of primitive mental conditions and as a deviation from the normal. We see much more clearly that affective action gives rise to therapeutic and developmental difficulties than that it also gives an impetus for mastering reality. Yet we do know the crucial role of affectivity in organizing and facilitating many ego functions; Freud (1937) implied this when he said that analysis is not expected to free man of all passions.

It would be easy to give further examples, but I will mention only one more—the application of psychoanalysis to the social sciences—which I think demonstrates particularly clearly that the concept of adaptation is indispensable to our theory and that the conflict-free ego sphere must be included in our studies. We hold that psychoanalysis is one of the basic sciences of sociology. Waelder (1936a) has recently discussed its significance for special problems of social sciences. Psychoanalysis and sociology have different centers of interest; many problems relevant in sociology are peripheral in psychoanalysis. Sociology centers on social action, on success or failure in the tasks set by society (i.e., tasks of adaptation); and is interested in the psychology of conflicts, the fate of aggressive and libidinal impulses, etc., only in so far as these are manifested in social behavior. What matters in sociology is man as an achiever (in the broadest sense of this word); it studies primarily what the mental apparatus achieves, and only indirectly how it masters its difficulties. For psychology, both conflict and achievement are indispensable points of view. The application of psychoanalysis to sociology coordinates these two points of view. We hope that the study of the conflict-free ego sphere and of its functions—and the further exploration of the problem of adaptation—will open up the no-man's land between sociology and psychoanalysis and thus extend the contribution of psychoanalysis to the social sciences. The probability of this is readily demonstrable, but I cannot give concrete examples here.

2.

Adaptation

So far I have pleaded for an extension of the psychoanalytic theory of ego development, and have attempted to show where this should begin. This extension and the concepts of ego functions that it implies (to be discussed later on) are rooted in and suggested by our present psychoanalytic conception of the ego. Clearly, such an extension could be based on a discussion of single cases or concrete situations. The advantage of the theoretical approach over the discussion of many-faceted concrete phenomena is, if nothing else, its brevity.

In what follows, I did not—and could not—attempt to pace out systematically the broad area of adaptation problems which are significant for psychoanalytic theory. Where my formulations appear one-sided or incomplete, it should be remembered that I had to make choices. The overemphasis of certain matters does not imply that I overlooked the others or that I thought them irrelevant.

The consideration of the conflict-free ego sphere leads us to the functions which are more or less closely related to the tasks of reality mastery, that is, *adaptation*. Now adaptation—though we do not discuss its implications frequently or thoroughly—is a central concept of psychoanalysis, because many of our problems, when pursued far enough, converge on it.

ADAPTATION

The concept of adaptation, though it appears simple, implies (or if crudely used, conceals) a great many problems. The analysis of this concept promises to clarify many problems of normal and abnormal psychology, among them our conception of mental health. Freud used "biological" concepts at crucial points of his theory (though he did not accept *wholesale* that so-called objective point of view which leads to behaviorism). For this reason, we believe, the psychoanalytic method "can be useful to the biologist in raising new problems which otherwise would escape his attention" (Schilder, 1933).

Generally speaking, we call a man well adapted if his productivity, his ability to enjoy life, and his mental equilibrium are undisturbed. In turn, we occasionally encounter statements ascribing any failure to a lack of adaptation. Such statements are meaningless because they overlook the relationship implied in the concept of adaptation, and thus beg the question: What makes a person succeed or fail in a given situation? The degree of adaptiveness can only be determined with reference to environmental situations (average expectable—i.e., typical—situations, or on the average not expectable—i.e., atypical—situations). We know very well how difficult it actually is to assess correctly the stability of the mental apparatus. Only the psychoanalytic process, and often not even that, can do it unequivocally (cf. Freud, 1937). Nothing less than a precise analysis of the adaptation concept and a more detailed knowledge of the adaptation processes will provide us with useful criteria.

The concept of adaptation has the most varied connotations in biology, and it has no precise definition in psychoanalysis either. For decades it was a cherished—perhaps all too cherished—concept of the biological sciences, but recently it has been frequently criticized and rejected. The observation underlying the concept "adaptation" is that living organisms patently "fit" into their environment. Thus, adaptation is primarily a reciprocal relationship between the organism and its environment. "Where the real functions, determined jointly by the organism's whole mechanism and by its environment, are favorable for its survival, there a relationship of adaptation obtains between that organism and its environment" (A. E. Parr, 1926, p. 3). We may distinguish between a *state of adaptedness* which obtains between the organism and its environment, and the *process of adaptation* which brings that state about. We may say that the entire development of these processes brings about a relationship, between the genotype and the environment, which is favorable for survival. A state of adaptedness may refer to the present and to the future. The process of adaptation always implies reference to a future condition; and we do not mean here the so-called negative limit of adaptation due to natural selection, and the like. At this point we encounter the controversies about the relation of phylogenesis to adaptation and the solutions proposed by Darwinism, Lamarckism, and other biological theories. These theories, however, have no direct bearing on our problem. We can even bypass Uexküll's biology, its critique of the adaptation concept based on the inherent planfulness of all organisms, and its preference for the theoretically less loaded concept of "fitting in."[1] Psychoanalysis enables us to discern those processes which by directly and actively changing either the environment or the person bring about a state of adaptedness between the individual and his environment; and to investigate the relationships between the preformed means of human adaptedness and these adaptation processes. We will clarify matters if we as-

[1] ["Fitting in" translates *Einpassung*.—*Tr*.]

ADAPTATION

sume that adaptation (speaking now mainly about man) is guaranteed, in both its grosser and finer aspects, on the one hand by man's primary equipment and the maturation of his apparatuses, and on the other hand by those ego-regulated actions which (using this equipment) counteract the disturbances in, and actively improve the person's relationship to, the environment. Man's existing relation to the environment codetermines which of the reactions he is capable of will be used in this process, and also which of the reactions used will predominate. The potentialities and the factual limitations of adaptation processes are already implied here.

I have indicated that familiar processes often, though naturally not always, appear in a new light when they are considered from the point of view of adaptation. The function of a behavior in the service of adaptation should be distinguished from its other possible functions, and often even from its genesis. For instance, the question "What is the adaptive achievement of expressive movements?" must be distinguished from "How do expressive movements come about?"; likewise, the function of anxiety as—according to Freud (1926b)—an indispensable biological reaction to danger must be distinguished from its ontogenesis in the individual. In many other instances it is naturally just this relationship to ontogeny or phylogeny that becomes the problem.

Here we must also keep in mind the phenomenon of "change of function," the role of which in mental life and particularly in the development of the ego seems to be very great, and behind which, genetically, there is always a particularly interesting bit of history. The conception of change of function is familiar in psychoanalysis: a behavior-form which originated in a certain realm of life may, in the course of development, appear in an entirely different realm and role.[2] An attitude which arose originally in the service of defense against an instinctual drive may, in the course of time, become an independent structure, in which case the instinctual drive merely triggers this automatized apparatus (more about this later on), but, as long as the automatization is not controverted, does not determine the details of its action. Such an apparatus may, as a relatively independent structure, come to serve other functions (adaptation, synthesis, etc.); it may also—and this is genetically of even broader significance—through a change of function turn from a means into a goal in its own right.[3] To write a psychoanalytic developmental history of "goals" from this point of view would be a rewarding endeavor. The problem of change of function has a technical aspect too, but I will not discuss that here.

Adaptation may come about by changes which the individual effects in his environment (use of tools, technology in the widest sense of the word, etc.), as well as by appropriate changes in his psychophysical system. Here Freud's concepts of alloplastic and autoplastic change are apposite. Animals, too, change their environment actively and purposefully, for example, by building nests and dens. A broad range of alloplastic adaptations is, however, available only to man. Two processes may be involved here: human action adapts the environment to human functions, and then the human being

[2] [The considerations presented here led to the concept of the "secondary autonomy of the ego." See "Comments on the Psychoanalytic Theory of the Ego." *The Psychoanalytic Study of the Child*, 5:74-96. New York: International Universities Press, 1950; "The Mutual Influences in the Development of Ego and Id." *The Psychoanalytic Study of the Child*, 7:9-30. New York: International Universities Press, 1952; and "Notes on the Theory of Sublimation." *The Psychoanalytic Study of the Child*, 10:9-29. New York: International Universities Press, 1955.]

[3] [For a further discussion of the psychological functions of goals, see "On Rational and Irrational Action." *Psychoanalysis and the Social Sciences*, 1:359-392. New York: International Universities Press, 1947.]

ADAPTATION

adapts (secondarily) to the environment which he has helped to create. Learning to act alloplastically is certainly one of the outstanding tasks of human development; yet alloplastic action is actually not always adaptive, nor is autoplastic action always unadaptive. It is often a higher ego function which decides whether an alloplastic or an autoplastic action—and in either case, what specific alteration—is appropriate in a given situation. Actually, however, instinctual drives and related factors always play a role too. Furthermore, the choice of the preferred means of adaptation may also be described crudely in typological terms (Kretschmer, 1921; Jung, 1920). A third form of adaptation, neither quite independent from nor quite identical with the alloplastic and autoplastic forms, is the choice of a new environment which is advantageous for the functioning of the organism. Parr attributes a crucial role to this form in his theory of "adaptiogenesis." I have already indicated that finding new, advantageous environments is of the greatest significance, particularly in human adaptation.

Individual adaptation—our sole concern so far—may clash with the adaptation of the species. At breeding time other "spheres of function" (Uexküll, 1920) recede and the individual becomes helpless against attack. Some species survive by virtue of their fecundity, while their individuals are poorly equipped for self-preservation. Many species display mutual assistance; in these the adaptation of the species and individual self-preservation clearly dovetail. Thus the adaptation of the individual and of the species are often but not always incompatible. Similar conditions exist in human society also, and psychoanalysis must take them into account when it deals with social matters. In setting therapeutic goals the individual's interests will generally outrank society's, but this will no longer hold when we have broadened our point of view to include the needs of society. Conversely, an individual's natural characteristics which do not coincide with his own interests, etc., may be important for society. This is certainly true for the existing societies; whether it must remain true for all ideal forms of society, can well be left an unanswered question.

We may not yet fully appreciate how fruitful it is that the foundation on which Freud built his theory of neurosis is not "specifically human" but "generally biological," so that for us the differences between animal and man (whether they be characterized as insightful action, or speech, or use of tools, or whatever) are relative. Let us examine some of these relative differences and consider their bearing on the problem of adaptation. Freud (1926b) contributed significantly to the answer when he enumerated the three outstanding factors which "play a part in the causation of neuroses and that have created the conditions under which the forces of the mind are pitted against one another" (p. 139): the prolonged helplessness and dependence of the human child, the latency period, and the fact that the ego must treat certain instinctual drives as dangers. He characterized one of these as a biological, one as a phylogenetic, and one as a purely psychological factor. The inherent antagonism of the ego toward instinctual drives described by Anna Freud (1936), and the fact that it is generally possible for instinctual drives, once they have been inhibited, to subserve adaptation, may also be pertinent here. Probably none of these factors is unique to man. For instance, some delay in the development of independence is demonstrable in all higher animals; Freud (1915b, p. 121) ascribed a differentiation of ego and id to other organisms also; and there are some indications of a latency period in apes too (Hermann, 1933). Nevertheless, the fact that all these factors are especially pronounced in man cannot be over-

ADAPTATION

looked. It is of particular importance for us that the prolonged helplessness of the human child is related to the fact that man acquires a crucial part of his adaptation processes by learning. Though the newborn human child is not devoid of all "instinct equipment"[4] (for instance, sucking, swallowing, eye closure on light stimulation, crying), nor of additional inborn equipment (instinctual drives and ego apparatuses) much of which matures only later, the fact remains that in comparison to other animals the "instinct equipment"[5] the newborn human has ready for use is extremely meager. In his prolonged helplessness the human child is dependent on the family, that is, on a social structure which fulfills here—as elsewhere—"biological" functions also. From the parents' point of view, the care of the young is a case of "altruistic purposiveness" (Becher)—but this is naturally not something final and irreducible. Bolk (1926) regards the human child's prolonged dependence (and the related formation of the family) as the result of a general "retardation" of development in man. According to him, man ripens slowly, his maturity is protracted, and his senilization decelerated. Bolk's conception of retardation is related to his well-known "fetalization hypothesis." Bally (1933) has convincingly shown that the prerequisite of learning by play is a state in which "nourishment and protection against enemies" are assured; and his attempt to derive the phylogenesis of man's mind from the evolution of the motor apparatus led him to believe that the protracted parental care is one of the causes of this evolution. The fact, stressed by Anna Freud, that for the small child the external world is a strong ally against his

---

[4] [The term "instinct" is used here in the sense of animal psychology: it translates the German term *Instinkt*. The psychoanalytic term *Trieb* is translated here as "instinctual drive."—*Tr.*]

[5] [See footnote 4 above.—*Tr.*]

instinctual drives, is also related to the extensive parental care.

The processes of adaptation are influenced both by constitution and external environment, and more directly determined by the ontogenetic phase of the organism. This developmental-historical factor in the process of adaptation has been particularly stressed by psychoanalysis. The term "historical reaction basis" (Driesch, 1908) seems applicable to it. Man does not come to terms with his environment anew in every generation; his relation to the environment is guaranteed by—besides the factors of heredity—an evolution peculiar to man, namely, the influence of tradition and the survival of the works of man. We take over from others (prototypes, tradition) a great many of our methods for solving problems (Bernfeld [1930] discussed this in regard to a special problem, and Laforgue [1937] recently investigated it in some detail). The works of man objectify the methods he has discovered for solving problems and thereby become factors of continuity, so that man lives, so to speak, in past generations as well as in his own. Thus arises a network of identifications and ideal-formations which is of great significance for the forms and ways of adaptation. Freud (1932) has shown the important role of the superego in this process: "... it becomes the vehicle of tradition and of all the age-long values, and transmits them from generation to generation" (p. 95). But the ego, too, has its share in building tradition. Whether these traditional methods of solution are rigid or modifiable depends on a great many individual and social factors. We know that in primitive societies they tend to be rigid.

What is the structure of the external world to which the human organism adapts? At this point we cannot separate biological from social conceptions. I do not want to go into the possible analogies to the social life of animals. The first social relations of the child are crucial for the maintenance of his biological equilibrium also. It is for this reason that man's first object relations became our main concern in psychoanalysis. Thus the task of man to adapt to man is present from the very beginning of life. Furthermore, man adapts to an environment part of which has not, but part of which has already been molded by his kind and himself. Man not only adapts to the community but also actively participates in creating the conditions to which he must adapt. Man's environment is molded increasingly by man himself. Thus the crucial adaptation man has to make is to the social structure, and his collaboration in building it. This adaptation may be viewed in various of its aspects and from various points of view; here we are focusing on the fact that the structure of society, the process of division of labor, and the social locus of the individual (cf. Bernfeld, 1931) codetermine the possibilities of adaptation and also regulate in part the elaboration of instinctual drives and the development of the ego. The structure of society decides (particularly—but not exclusively—through its effect on education) which forms of behavior shall have the greatest adaptive chance. Each situation will require different (some more, and some less specialized) forms of behavior, achievements, forms of life and equilibria. We may describe the fact that the social structure determines, at least in part, the adaptive chances of a particular form of behavior, by the term *social compliance,* coined in analogy to "somatic compliance."[6] Social compliance is a special form of the environmental "compliance" which is implied by the concept of adaptation. This social compliance plays a role not only

[6] [For a more detailed discussion, see "The Application of Psychoanalytic Concepts to Social Science." *Psa. Quart.,* 19:385-392, 1950; also in *The Yearbook of Psychoanalysis,* 7:81-87. New York: International Universities Press, 1951.]

in the development of neurosis, psychopathy and criminality (though it by no means suffices to explain them) but also in normal development and particularly in the earliest social organization of the child's environment. It is a special instance of social compliance when society, so to speak, corrects an adaptation disturbance: individual propensities which amount to disturbances of adaptation in one social group or locus may fulfill a socially essential function in another. It is often overlooked that the degree of need gratification and particularly the possibilities for development afforded by a given social order may not have parallel influences on the child and on the adult. It may not be superfluous to mention again that by adaptation we do not mean only passive submission to the goals of society, but also active collaboration on them and attempts to change them.

I discuss these familiar themes here merely to demonstrate the multiple layering of man's adaptation processes. In judging the degree of a person's adaptation—which is the implied basis of our concept of health—many factors must be taken into account, the concrete forms of which we are in many cases not yet familiar with.[7]

I believe I am in harmony with Freud's conception when I stress simultaneously the primary importance of social factors in human development and their biological significance. Freud's view united the biological and sociological points of view. In contrast to this, we have now within psychoanalysis the familiar split between a more "biological" and a more "sociological" view of normal and pathological development. Neither the extreme view in which development is a matter of instinctual drives and the influence of the external world

[7] [Cf. "Psychoanalysis and the Concept of Health." *Int. J. Psa.*, 20:308-321, 1939.]

is insufficiently regarded (I once called it "biological solipsism"), nor its "sociological" counterpart (cf. Waelder, 1936b) corresponds to Freud's point of view. However, the terms we use here, including my "biological solipsism," are questionable: they more or less equate sociological with environmental and biological with nonenvironmental. The use of the term "environmental" is understandable, but why biological and "nonenvironmental" should be equated is hard to understand. Is the relationship of the child to his mother, or the care of children not a biological process? Have we the right to exclude the processes of adaptation from biology? Biological functions and environmental relationships are not in antithesis. This is not merely a terminological correction: the terms imply an underestimation of the very areas of biology with which we are concerned here. It seems to me that here the facts cannot be separated into biological and sociological, though we are entitled to study them now more in the context of biology and now more in the context of sociology. But in psychoanalysis we often use the term biological to contrast the anatomical or the physiological with the psychological. We say, for instance, that infantile sexuality and the latency period have a biological foundation; thereby referring, for instance, to the anatomical-physiological fact that the development of the female "germa" (Bolk) is completed by the fourth or fifth year of life, whereafter a pause in development follows which corresponds to a physiological inhibition. Likewise, when we say that the transition from one phase of libido organization to the next is biologically predetermined, we are again referring to physiological processes. It is probably in a similar sense that the id and the ego are incorrectly contrasted as the biological and the nonbiological components of personality. Here the term biological is used not only as anatomical-physiological, but also, in the above-stated sense, as "nonenvironmental," in contrast to the ego's relatedness to the environment. There would be no objection against this usage either, were it not that it clashes with the emphasis psychoanalysis—in contrast to other psychologies—puts on the biological function of the mind, including thinking, consciousness, etc. In our opinion the psychological is not an "antithesis" to the biological, but rather an essential part of it. Psychology and biology are for us simply two different directions of work, two points of view, two methods of investigation, and two sets of concepts. Moreover, it must be remembered that psychoanalysis does use biological concepts, in the here defined sense. The ambiguity is no doubt related to the position psychoanalytic theory allots to the instinctual drive: Freud (1915a) defined it as a borderline concept between the psychological and organic. Accordingly, at times we contrast the concept of instinctual drive to the soma, and at other times we describe somatic changes as processes involving instinctual drives (and not just as sequelae of such processes). These comments merely supplement Bibring's (1936) discussion of the fluid relationship, in psychoanalytic theory, between instinctual drive and mental apparatus.

This distinction between a biological and a psychological *point of view* raises another important question: Can psychoanalysis, with its psychological methods of investigation and with its predominantly psychological concepts, trace physiological processes of development? We reject the customary form of this question: What is biological and what is psychological in the developmental process? We ask instead: What part of it is congenital, what maturational, and what environmentally determined? What physiological and what psychological changes take place in it? Our psychological method encompasses more than just the processes of mental development. Precisely because the psychological is a part of the biological, under certain conditions our method sheds light on physiological developments, particularly on those pertaining to instinctual drives. We can trace the course of these developments, using psychological phenomena as their indicator or symptom. This relationship has still another aspect: for instance, though we can describe the differences between masculine and feminine to some extent psychologically, it does not follow that there must be fundamental psychological concepts which correspond to masculinity and femininity. But the relation of the "psychological" and the "biological" is further complicated by their interplay with the endogenous and exogenous. Here the most important question is: Are the exogenous factors the average expectable kind (family situation, mother-child relationship and others), or are they environmental conditions of a different sort? In other words, the question is whether, and to what extent, a certain course of development *can count on average expectable stimulations* (environmental releasers) and whether, and to what extent, and in what direction, it will be deflected by environmental influences of a different sort. Here I have distinguished two kinds of exogenous factors. Following this trend of thought would lead us into a discussion of the factors which, in the average case, guarantee normal development, development to health, but I will not pursue the matter any further. I would like to refer only to a passage in Freud's "The Passing of the Oedipus Complex" (1924b) which is in accord with the view I have presented here on the heuristic potential of psychoanalysis in regard to these problems. Discussing the question whether the decline of the Oedipus complex is determined by heredity or by certain experiences, Freud said: "Even at birth, indeed, the whole organism is destined to die, and an indication of what will eventually cause its death may possibly already be contained in its organic disposition. Yet after all it is of interest to follow up the way in which the innate schedule is worked out, the way in which accidental noxiae exploit the disposition" (p. 270).

We return now to the problems of adaptation proper. Within the limits of this study I cannot analyze more precisely either the pathways of adaptation or those by which the correction of adaptation disturbances takes place. Some of these are familiar to all of us and for the analysis of others we lack the prerequisites. Here I would like to contrast only two forms of adaptation, which often—though as we shall see, not always—differ greatly in their premises and consequences. I refer to what might be termed *progressive* and *regressive* adaptations. The term progressive adaptation is self-explanatory; it is an adaptation whose direction coincides with that of development. But there are adaptations—successful ones, and not mere unsuccessful attempts—which use pathways of regression. I do not refer only to the well-known fact that the genetic roots of even rational and adapted behavior are irrational, but rather to those highly adapted purposeful achievements of healthy people which—the generally justified contrasting of regressive and adapted behavior to the contrary notwithstanding—require a detour through regression. The reason for this is that the function of the most highly differentiated organ of reality adaptation cannot alone guarantee an optimal total adaptation of the organism. This is related to the problem of "fitting together" and particularly to the fact that the general plan even of successful adaptation processes often includes regulations which are not specifically adaptive. More about all this further below. There is, for example, the detour through fantasy. Though fantasy is always rooted in the past, it can, by connecting past and future, become the basis for realistic goals. There are the symbolic images familiar in productive scientific thinking; and there are poetry and all the other forms of artistic activity and experience. On the relation of these processes to the synthetic function of the ego, more will be said below. Kris (1934) speaks of these in terms of a "regression in the service of the ego."

3.

Adaptation and "Fitting Together"—The Reality Principle

THE RELATIONSHIP of the individual to his environment is "disrupted" from moment to moment and must again and again be returned to an equilibrium. The "equilibrium" is not necessarily normal; it may be pathological. (It would be meaningless to call every disruption of equilibrium a conflict. This would rob the concept of all precision. Every stimulus disrupts the equilibrium, but not every stimulus causes conflict. These processes therefore occur partly in the conflict-free sphere.) Apparently every organism has mechanisms for maintaining or re-establishing equilibrium.[1] We can picture the process as an oscillation around the equilibrium. It is not that every process in the organism must subserve the individual's survival: the biological task of procreation may supersede that aim, and the theory of the death instinct postulates regulatory processes whose aim is different. E. Bibring has rightly stated that Freud's theory implies both forms of regulation: "The life system is governed by two trends: it moves towards zero potential but in doing so it creates new tensions" (1936, p. 122). R. Ehrenberg's (1923)

[1] [Cf. "Comments on the Psychoanalytic Theory of Instinctual Drives." *Psa. Quart.*, 17:368-388, 1948.]

ingenious monistic conception of life as a process directed toward death is well known. Of course, tensions also arise within the organism itself, and not only in its relations to the outside world. I will assume that the relationships of these tensions to the Freudian regulation principles (pleasure principle, reality principle, nirvana principle), and the relationships of the repetition compulsion to the instinctual drives and to the ability to regenerate, and so forth, are well known. I need not mention here how the repetition compulsion may serve adaptation, as in traumatic neuroses.

Here we are interested in the mental states of equilibrium, in their stability, and particularly in their relationship to the environment. We must stress the great elasticity of human adaptiveness: there are always several alternative means available to master an environmental relationship. But psychoanalytic experience has also taught us that because of the complex structure of the mental apparatus, internal disturbances readily cause disturbances in the relation to reality. Our knowledge of the mental apparatus enables us to discern, besides the equilibrium between individual and environment, two other relatively well-defined states of equilibrium. These, the equilibrium of instinctual drives (vital equilibrium) and the equilibrium of mental institutions (structural equilibrium), are dependent on each other and on the first-mentioned equilibrium (cf. Freud, 1931; and Alexander, 1933). Actually, however, we must add a fourth equilibrium. Since the ego is not merely a resultant of other forces, its synthetic function is, so to speak, a specific organ of equilibrium at the disposal of the person. The fourth equilibrium is between the synthetic function and the rest of the ego. We will return to this point later.

Here we have come upon the interdependence of the regulators of intrapsychic equilibrium. (The psychoanalytic study of those primary disorders of ego apparatuses which result in failures of adaptation has barely begun.) The same process which is "internally" a disturbance in the relation of the mental institutions may be "externally" a disturbance of adaptation: for instance, defense against instinctual drives often alters the relationships to the external world. Biology speaks of an "organization of the organism" by which it means "the lawful correlation of the organism's individual parts" (A. E. Parr, 1926). We are justified in saying that *adaptation* and *fitting together*[2] (in the sense of this correlation) are interdependent; fitting together is usually the prerequisite of an adaptation process and vice versa. This correlation also includes the psychophysical relations, and its psychological expression is the synthetic function (cf. Nunberg, 1930), which is thus a special case of the broader biological concept of fitting together.[3] Here—as so often in biology—on a higher level the same tasks are solved by different means. In phylogenesis, evolution leads to an increased independence of the organism from its environment, so that reactions which originally occurred in relation to the external world are increasingly displaced into the interior of the organism. The development of thinking, of the superego, of the mastery of internal danger before it becomes external, and so forth, are examples of this process of internalization. Thus fitting together (in the psychological realm, the synthetic function) gains in significance in the course of evolution. If we encounter—as we do in man—a function which simultaneously regulates both the environmental relationships and the interrelations of the mental institutions, we will have to place it above adaptation in the

[2] [The German terms are *Anpassung* and *Zusammenpassung.—Tr.*]
[3] [Cf. "On Rational and Irrational Action." *Psychoanalysis and the Social Sciences,* 1:359-392. New York: International Universities Press, 1947.]

biological hierarchy: we will place it above adaptive activity regulated by the external world, that is, above adaptation in the narrower sense, but not above adaptation in the broader sense, because the latter already implies a "survival value," determined both by the environmental relationships and the interrelations of mental institutions.

Let us now return to the principles of regulation. At this point we are interested only in that one of their aspects which can help us to demonstrate the relative independence of ego development. Thus we may disregard for the moment the role of the repetition compulsion and of the nirvana principle in development. There are undoubtedly reactions in which the pleasure principle serves self-preservation: for example, biologically, the widespread role of pain (as a warning) seems to be primarily to prevent self-mutilation (Uexküll, 1920). Rats will eat their own legs when the sensory nerves in them have been cut. Yet, as Freud (1932) put it, "From the pleasure principle to the instinct of self-preservation is a long way; and the two tendencies are far from coinciding from the first" (p. 129). Psychoanalysis has impressed upon us how much the pleasure principle disturbs adaptation, and this can easily lead us to underestimate its significance in the mastery of the external world.[4] Since Freud's "Two Principles" (1911) we know how and within what limits the reality principle replaces or modifies the pleasure principle in man. In another and no less fundamental study, "Negation" (1925), Freud continues these considerations and discusses the foundations of reality testing and the relationship of thinking to perception (cf. also Ferenczi, 1926). But how the pleasure principle was, so to speak, forced to modify into the

[4] [These issues are treated more explicitly in "Notes on the Reality Principle." *The Psychoanalytic Study of the Child*, 11:31-53. New York: International Universities Press, 1956.]

reality principle has still not been explained unequivocally.

We understand that the mental apparatus must search the external world for pleasure possibilities as soon as its needs exceed a certain measure and can no longer be satisfied by fantasy. The turning to reality can also be a protection against anxieties aroused by fantasies and may serve to master anxiety. In these two cases the turning to the external world and the necessity to acknowledge it are still completely under the sway of the pleasure principle. The person trades pleasure for displeasure or a greater pleasure for a lesser one. But what we call the reality principle implies something essentially new, namely the function of *anticipation*. "A momentary pleasure, uncertain in its result, is given up, but only in order to gain in the new way an assured pleasure coming later" (Freud, 1911, p. 18). As Nunberg (1932) has correctly said, the child renounces his omnipotence and magic only in the hope that he will regain them when he grows up. (Similar occurences are frequent in the course of psychoanalytic treatment.) We know that the reality principle is, in a sense, a continuation of the pleasure principle, but its means are different. But the reality principle has another crucial implication besides the increased regard for the external world. The ability to renounce an immediate pleasure-gain in order to secure a greater one in the future cannot be derived from the pleasure principle alone; not even memories of painful experiences suffice to explain it. It is in this connection that Ferenczi (1926) raised the problem of the willing acceptance of actual pain. Masochism, which he invoked as the explanation, does at times seem to play a role in this; for instance, in the restitution process following the schizophrenic's loss of hold on reality (Nunberg, 1932). But it seems improbable that masochism should have a central role in the adaptation processes of normal development. Nor can the repetition compulsion, invoked by French's (1937) relevant paper, alone explain this reference to a future event. The repetition compulsion can certainly account for some of our pain experiences, but its relation to the reality principle is far less direct than he assumes it to be. Though the content of French's conception contradicts Ferenczi's masochism hypothesis, they are similar in one respect: the masochistic attitude, like the repetition compulsion, cannot *by itself* guarantee adaptation to reality; it can do so only if we have already assumed that it will not become effective except when the development of a reality relationship demands acceptance of pain. We cannot consider adaptive a relationship to the world in which we take cognizance of the world only in so far as it causes pain.

But we have already indicated that the reality principle also implies something essentially new, namely the familiar *function of anticipating* the future, orienting our actions according to it and correctly relating means and ends to each other. It is an ego function and, surely, an adaptation process of the highest significance. We may assume that ego development enters this process as an independent variable, though naturally the ego function involved may secondarily yield pleasure. We shall soon have more to say about the "principle" which regulates this part of ego development.

This state of affairs may be of general significance. We may ask why certain modes of behavior have greater *pleasure potentialities* than others. Clearly, the psychology of instinctual drives does not completely answer this question. Ferenczi (1924) assumes that the extraordinarily great narcissistic cathexis of the penis is due to its role in the propagation of the species. We must not hesitate to generalize this assumption and include general biological considerations of this kind in explaining the pleasure potentialities of an organ or behavior. The requirements for the survival of the species can take a form, in the mental development of man, which may be independent from the pleasure principle—and from a reality principle that is secondarily derived from it—and can even regulate the possibilities of pleasure gain. A similar assumption may be made for the needs of self-preservation: for instance, the libidinal activity of the oral zone "leans," to begin with, upon the alimentary need. We may have before us a relationship to the external world which, as an independent factor, regulates certain prerequisites of the application of the pleasure principle. Thus we arrive at a conception in which relations to reality are determined by a *reality principle in the broader* and a *reality principle in the narrower sense.* (Whether or not the first of these, which includes effects of natural selection, hereditary influences, etc., can still be considered one of the regulative principles in our usual sense, is a question which I do not want to bring in here.) The reality principle in the broader sense would historically precede and hierarchically outrank the pleasure principle. The subordination of the pleasure principle to the reality principle, in this sense, was discussed by Rado (1931). I do not think it unwarranted trespassing to propose such a broadening of the concept of the reality principle. We are so accustomed to general biological conceptions in psychoanalysis—the psychoanalytic classification of instinctual drives, for instance, essentially rests on biological considerations—that there should be a place in it for this conception too. We have here, so to speak, two levels of theory-formation, just as in the psychoanalytic theory of instinctual drives, where the instinctual drive-processes we deal with in our psychoanalytic work are on one level, and the general biological derivation of the death instinct, the application of the libido theory to the relation of cells to each other, etc., are on the other level. While there certainly are relations between the broader and the narrower reality principle, nevertheless, at the present stage of research it is advisable to indicate the level of discourse each time, in order to avoid misunderstanding. At this point I would like to quote a statement of Freud which may support the point of view developed here: "Both higher development and involution might well be the consequences of adaptation to the pressure of external forces; and in both cases the part played by instincts might be limited to the retention (in the form of an internal source of pleasure) of an obligatory modification" (1920, p. 41).

We have seen that the change of the pleasure principle into the reality principle in the narrower sense presupposes a certain level of ego development. Doubts certainly will arise about the generalization of such considerations; because, while psychoanalysis, in considering phylogenesis, readily attributes a broad and even primary role to the influence of the external world—to the "dire necessities of life"—in the formation and the function of organs, it does not, in general, have a high opinion of the individual's inborn adaptive abilities as guarantees of successful reality relationships and of mastery of the environment. (I will not discuss here Ferenczi's [1924] thoughtful and, in its approach certainly consistent, "bioanalysis"; in general, I agree with Bernfeld's [1937] recent critique.) Our long neglect of this factor is due partly to a lack of means to deal with it and partly to the fact that the instinctual drive aspect of mental processes engaged our interest much earlier than their ego aspect. A methodological note: the concept of adaptation (as a process) probably arose as a generalization from observations of individual human adaptive activities, and therefore, when applied to the ontogenesis of adaptation processes, it is less loaded with hypotheses than when it is applied to phylogenesis.

We know that, according to Freud, the development of the upright posture had a decisive influence on the vicissitudes of man's instinctual drives. Why shouldn't we then—keeping in mind the differences between ontogenetic and phylogenetic situations—assume a similar relationship between adaptation and instinctual drive in ontogenesis as well? No instinctual drive in man guarantees adaptation in and of itself, yet on the average the whole ensemble of instinctual drives, ego functions, ego apparatuses, and the principles of regulation, as they meet the average expectable environmental conditions, do have survival value. Of these elements, the function of the ego apparatuses—about which more later—is "objectively" the most purposive. The proposition that the external world "compels" the organism to adapt can be maintained only if one already takes man's survival tendencies and potentialities for granted. (It is not within our scope to consider the phylogenetic question as to the role of natural selection in this, or the question whether or not "adaptive activities," in our sense, also play a role in it.)

The functions of all the mental and physical ego apparatuses mentioned can become secondarily sources of pleasure. This is apparently a "compensation" in the broader sense (cf. Tausk, 1913). The pleasure possibilities of the apparatuses of the conflict-free ego sphere seem, in any case, to play an important role in the adaptation to the external world, since the opening of such new sources of pleasure furthers ego development. (See discussion of pleasure in functioning below.) Let us consider first the somatic processes of maturation: just as the phases of libido development depend upon somatic maturation processes (for instance, the anal-sadistic phase develops "obviously in connection with the cutting of the teeth, the strengthening of the musculature, and the control of the sphincters" [Freud, 1932, p. 135]), so

ADAPTATION AND "FITTING TOGETHER"

ego development too is connected with the somatic maturation of certain apparatuses. I will have more to say about this later on. The sources and character of pleasure change in the course of ego development. The pleasure potentialities afforded at the various levels of development by the ego, its functions, and its apparatuses, are of great significance for the stability of ego organization, its effectiveness, and the kind and extent of its functioning (synthesis, defense, assimilation, learning ability, etc.). However, we know that the sexualization of ego activities may lead to their inhibition; and that the intactness of certain sexual functions (genital functions) is, up to a point, a guarantee against the interference of libidinal with utilitarian functions. What should follow here is the characterization and qualitative differentiation of the various categories of pleasure experiences—not a simple task. First, those feelings of pleasure which have strong somatic reverberations (primarily the sexual ones) could be distinguished from the pleasure qualities of the aim-inhibited, sublimated activities. But even these could be further subdivided, as in Scheler's (1927) classification: sensory feelings or experience feelings; somatic and vital feelings; pure psychic feelings (pure self-feelings); mental feelings (personality feelings).[5]

---

[5] [The terms listed here render Max Scheler's (1927, particularly p. 344ff.) following terms in sequence: *sinnliche Gefühle, Empfindungsgefühle, Leibgefühle, Lebensgefühle, seelische Gefühle (Ichgefühle), geistige Gefühle (Persönlichkeitsgefühle).—Tr.*]

4.

Ego Development and Adaptation

To ASSUME that all reactions to the external world are processes of adaptation would increase the vagueness of this concept; nevertheless, an attempt should be made to restudy the evolution of the ego in terms of adaptation. We do attribute a sort of ego to animals also (Freud, 1915b, p. 121). The animal is in contact with the external world by means of its receptors and effectors, it develops a "world of percepts" (*"Merkwelt"*), a "world of action" (*"Wirkwelt"*), and by "exerting regulative functions" it also creates an "internal world" (Uexküll, 1920). But we cannot speak, in regard to the animal, of that kind of separation into ego and id which exists in the human adult. The very fact that the concept of instincts as it pertains to the lower animals is much more comprehensive than the concept of instinctual drives as it pertains to man prevents such a separation. It is possible, and even probable, that it is just this sharper differentiation of the ego and the id—the more precise division of labor between them—in human adults which on the one hand makes for a superior, more flexible, relation to the external world, and on the other *increases the alienation of the id from reality*.[1]

[1] [Cf. "Comments on the Psychoanalytic Theory of Instinctual Drives." *Psa. Quart.*, 17:368-388, 1948; and "Notes on the Theory of Aggression" (with Ernst Kris & Rudolph M. Loewenstein). *The Psychoanalytic Study of the Child*, 3/4:9-36. New York: International Universities Press, 1949.]

In the animal neither of these two institutions is so flexibly close to or so alienated from reality. Perhaps we can assume that the pleasure principle is, on the average, more closely related to the preservation of the self and the species in the animal than in man. The assumption that lower organisms are regulated only by the pleasure principle (or the nirvana principle) is—in the form in which it is usually stated—certainly untenable, but it becomes more plausible if we assume that in lower animals reality relationships provide the patterns for the aims and means of pleasure-gain to a greater extent that they do in man. In this area we must be particularly cautious in drawing phylogenetic inferences from observations made on the human child.

The newborn infant is not wholly a creature of drives; he has inborn apparatuses (perceptual and protective mechanisms) which appropriately perform a part of those functions which, after the differentiation of ego and id, we attribute to the ego. A state of adaptedness exists before the intentional processes of adaptation begin. Man's particularly limited inventory of instincts,[2] and the great latitude this leaves for learning, have already been mentioned; but we cannot assume that the regulating factors and their relation to the external world begin to function only when the ego is fully developed. Even defenses, though not in the common and narrower sense, already exist on the level of instincts.[3] Ego development is a differentiation, in which these primitive regulating factors are increasingly replaced or supplemented by more effective ego regulations. What was originally anchored in instincts may subsequently be performed in the service of and by means of the ego, though, naturally, new regulations too will arise in the course of the development

[2] [See footnote 4 on p. 29.—*Tr.*]
[3] [See footnote 4 on p. 29.—*Tr.*]

of the ego and the id. Differentiation progresses not only by the creation of new apparatuses to master new demands and new tasks, but also and mainly by new apparatuses taking over, on a higher level, functions which were originally performed by more primitive means. As an aside I will mention a consequence of this: when superordinate apparatuses are blocked or disordered, no pure form of a previous developmental stage emerges. This is so in the organic realm and—though for well-known reasons to a lesser degree (cf. Freud, 1930)—in the psychological realm also.

We customarily assume that mental development is determined both by instinctual drives and environmental influences, and that this holds also for the development of the ego (the specific organ of adaptation) that is, the learning of ways to satisfy and to control instinctual drives. But we must not forget that the individual's drive constitution is not his only inborn equipment, that is, not the only "given" from the point of view of ontogenetic considerations. The human individual, at his birth, also has apparatuses, which serve to master the external world. These mature in the course of development.[4] We will discuss these apparatuses and their role as an independent factor in development in more detail later. (Part of Bally's [1933] revealing ideas on motility and evolution, and M. Löwy's [1928] investigations on the dependence of ego development on motility pertain to this point.) Moreover, the human individual possesses at his birth an as yet unexplored inventory of mental dispositions, comprising constitutional factors important in ego development; for instance, according to Brierley (1936), individual differ-

---

[4] [These considerations led to the concept of the "primary autonomy of the ego." Cf. "Comments on the Psychoanalytic Theory of the Ego." *The Psychoanalytic Study of the Child*, 5:74-96. New York: International Universities Press, 1950.]

ences of anxiety-tolerance are determined by such a constitutional factor. The ego's progressive learning in the course of development to tolerate anxieties and tensions has been extensively studied by ego psychology. Anna Freud, the English school, and Fenichel have presented much accumulated material of experience and thought about the development and function of the ego's goals and defense mechanisms, which I cannot discuss here in detail. I want to stress only the point I have made repeatedly, that defense processes may *simultaneously* serve both the control of instinctual drive and adaptation to the external world (Anna Freud's "identification with the aggressor" is an example). We observe at every turn that the ego simultaneously effects adaptation, inhibition, and synthesis. (The familiar analogy with certain parts of the central nervous system is obvious but helps us very little.)

Strictly speaking, the normal newborn human and his average expectable environment are adapted to each other from the very first moment. That no infant can survive under certain atypical (on the average not expectable) conditions and that traumata certainly are integral to typical development, do not contradict this proposition. This relationship is, however, in the main, *a state of adaptedness* (both for the present and for the future, as we shall soon see), and processes of adaptation in the narrower sense play almost no role as yet. In this sense the individual has a relationship to the external world from the very beginning. The newborn is in close touch with his environment not only by his need for its continuous care but also by his reactions to its stimuli; though, of course, these reactions are often not at first specifically adapted. The first signs of intentionality appear around the third month of life and mark a crucial phase of development, but true object comprehension makes a definite appearance only around the fifth or sixth month and is not complete even at the age of one year (cf. Ch. Bühler, 1928). We know something about the role of the child's needs in influencing and directing the development of intention phenomena, and I will not discuss this point here. But we should not assume, from the fact that the child and the environment interact from the outset, that the child is from the beginning psychologically directed toward the object as an object. M. Balint's (1937) assertions, and those of others, concerning *primary* object-love can hardly be reconciled with these easily verifiable findings. Balint argued that it is unjustified to use "the circumstance that an experience is not conscious, as proof against its mental existence." In general this is certainly true. Yet methodology warns us that, in a realm which is more amenable to direct observation than to reconstruction from the psychoanalysis of adults, we should avoid making assumptions which clash with observations of behavior. For a further discussion of these and other problems of early ego development, I must refer you to Fenichel (1937b) and Balint (1937), since I have merely touched on them here.

It is known that the structural development in the individual, too, serves adaptation. This is true by definition for the differentiation of the ego and the id, but it also holds for the identifications which build the superego, where the relationship between what is achievement and what disturbance in adaptation is particularly clear. If Rado (1925) chose to speak of a "conscience drive," we, in turn, must stress that such a "drive" has an adaptive function too. The superego is not only in antithesis to the ego and the id; it is also "to some extent an ideal prototype of that state toward which all the ego's endeavours are tending, a reconciliation of its manifold allegiances" (Freud, 1924a, p. 253); moreover, it is an outcome of an adaptation and its subserves synthesis (cf. Nunberg, 1930). We know, however, that structure development also increases the lability of the mental apparatus and, therefore, we must expect temporary (and occasionally enduring) dedifferentiation phenomena. In turn differentiations in the ego also create specific conditions for adaptation: the forms of adaptation depend, among other things, upon the mental level and on the wealth, scope and differentiation of the inner world. This differentiation within the ego leads to an optimal adaptation and synthesis only if the ego is strong and can use it freely; nevertheless, differentiation has an independent role among the adaptation processes. Differentiation is counteracted by a tendency toward a "closed world," which may be either an expression of the synthetic function in our sense (cf. Nunberg's [1930] analysis of the need for causality) or a regression to earlier developmental stages of "fitting together," to a feeling of being one with the object, to a primary narcissistic state (Rado, 1925; H. Deutsch, 1927; and others). Even this regressive tendency may, under certain conditions, serve adaptation. According to E. Sharpe (1935), for instance, thinking in "pure science" involves restitution tendencies. It goes without saying that thinking, and particularly causal thinking, implies not only synthesis and fitting together, but also differentiation. We are dealing here with the coexistence of *differentiation* and *integration* (cf. Werner, 1929), familiar in biology. The development of this function of differentiation finds psychological expression not only in the formation of the mental institutions, but also in reality testing, in judgment, in the extension of the world of perception and action, in the separation of perception from imagery, cognition from affect, etc. The equilibrium of these two functions may be disrupted, for instance, by precocity of differentiation, relative retardation of synthesis. When we speak of the precocity of ego development we often mean the precocity of these differentiation processes. Differentiation must be recognized, along with synthesis, as an important function of the ego. Spitz's (1936) recent lecture on differentiation and integration is relevant in this connection. Since we somehow connect the synthetic function of the ego with the libido (our conception of this relationship is unimportant here), it is plausible to assume an analogous relationship between differentiation and destruction, particularly since Freud's (1937) recent inferences about the role of free aggression in mental life. Once again, I cannot discuss either the well-known or the possible relationships between these developmental processes and the instinctual drives.

We have already mentioned that adaptation achievements may turn into adaptation disturbances. We know, for instance, that not all people can tolerate full compliance with the external world and its demands (for example, social demands); their synthetic function cannot keep pace, so to speak. We also know that the neurotic symptom, too, is an attempt at adaptation, though an abortive one. Such contradictions are apparently a necessary concomitant of biological evolution. In this connection Freud (1937) quotes Goethe: "Reason becomes unreason, kindness torment." No doubt many biological processes, purposive in and of themselves, also have deleterious side effects on the organism. Processes of adaptation are, first of all, purposive only for a certain range of environmental situations; moreover, they involve internal self-limiting factors, which may or may not be adaptive. Unicellular organisms when left to themselves are finally destroyed by the products of their metabolism. You will remember that Freud (1920) referred to this fact in his discussion of the death instinct. Conversely, adaptation disturbances may turn into adaptation achievements when appropriately elaborated. Normal development involves typical conflicts, and with them the possibility of adaptation disturbances.[5] Even though the concept of mental health must necessarily remain vague, Waelder in a recent discussion rightly said that mental health cannot be considered a product of chance. One of its premises is preparedness for *average expectable* environmental situations and for *average expectable* internal conflicts.

I believe we will find it easy to accept the idea that ego functions have, in addition to their coordination, *a rank order* as well. E. Weiss, for example (1937), spoke of superficial and deeper layers of defense, but this rank order need not coincide with the rank order of ego functions in terms of their biological purposiveness. We have seen, for instance, that fitting together, the synthetic function, must be supraordinate to the regulation by the external world. We will see later on that there are also rational regulations on higher and lower levels (concepts like intelligence, objectivation, causal thinking, and means-end relationships are some of these). Even the various aspects of the synthetic function have different degrees of biological significance. A big step in human development separates the primitive synthetic regulations which are at work in the formation of the superego from those synthetic achievements which are our goals in psychoanalytic treatment. The same holds for the differentiation function also. Psychoanalytic therapy may change the basis of this rank order by inducing a new division of labor: for instance, the ego may take over tasks which have previously been performed by other institutions. Much is still unclear in these matters, and will remain unclear until the development of the functions of the conflict-free ego sphere has been understood. This holds particularly for the psychology of psychoses

[5] [Cf. "Psychoanalysis and the Concept of Health." *Int. J. Psa.*, 20:308-321, 1939.]

(for schizophrenia but also for the so-called organic psychoses). What we do already know, however, is that a person's stability and effectiveness are decisively influenced by the purposive coordination and rank order of functions—in terms of adaptation, differentiation, and synthesis—*within* the ego, and not only by the plasticity or strength of instinctual drive, and the tolerance for tension, etc., in terms of which ego strength is usually defined. It is quite consistent with these considerations to speak of the primacy of the regulation by intelligence. A discussion of the concept of purposiveness would be in place here, but I cannot enter on it now.

5.

Internalization, Thinking, and Rational Behavior

In the course of evolution, described here as a process of progressive "internalization," there arises a central regulating factor, usually called the "inner world," which is interpolated between the receptors and the effectors. We are familiar with it in human adults as one of the ego's regulating factors. The breadth of the subjective world, the degree of sensitivity to experiences, etc., reflect individual differences in this factor. Here, however, we are not concerned with the inner world as such, but rather with its role in objective functional relationships.

Freud (1920) impressed on us the importance of the "stimulus barrier," which permits the transmission of "only a fragment of the original [stimulus] intensity" (p. 27) into the interior of the organism. But there is at first no such stimulus barrier against instinctual drives, and therefore displacements of drive stimulation are more significant in mental economy than are displacements of external stimulations. For this reason the biological functions of the inner world (and its relations to the environment) are easily disturbed by the instinctual drives. This closeness of the inner world to the instinctual drives has, however, a positive significance for adaptation also. The animal's picture of the external world narrows and broadens as the demands of his instincts become stronger or weaker; its center shifts, according to whether he is hungry, in heat, etc., to those elements which are directly related to the gratification of the instinct. In man this advantage is counteracted by the equivocal relation between instinctual drive and biological utility, but this very fact enhances the significance of the objectifying regulations.

The biological usefulness of the inner world in adaptation, in differentiation, and in synthesis becomes obvious even in a brief glance at the biological significance of thought processes. Perception, memory, imagery, thinking, and action are the relevant factors in this connection. (On the biological significance of imagery see K. Bühler, 1930.). The inner world and its functions make possible an adaptation process which consists of two steps: withdrawal from the external world and return to it with improved mastery. The fact that goals are not directly approached but reached by interpolated detours (means) is a decisive step in evolution. This withdrawal from reality the better to master it, which we will frequently encounter, is not identical with the "regressive adaptation" (in a genetic sense) which we discussed above. The development of consciousness does not fully coincide with the development of the inner world. Freud stressed the social significance of consciousness. Perhaps W. Stern (1914) is right when he suggests that consciousness arises as an expression of conflicts (Anna Freud's [1936, p. 179] comment that instinctual danger makes a human being intelligent may also be pertinent here).

The world of thought and the world of perception—both of which are among the ego's regulating factors and are elements of that adaptation process which consists of withdrawal for the purpose of mastery—need not always coincide. Perception and imagination orient us by means of spatial-temporal images. Thinking frees us from the immediate perceptual situation (memory and imagination are of course its precursors in this), and its highest form—in exact science—strives to exclude all images and qualities from its world. Psychoanalysis was the first psychology to make a serious attempt at a reduction of conscious qualities. Still, images do have, in many situations, a regulative role in human action. Both these worlds have a specific relation to action: not only thought implies an action tendency, the image does too, albeit a primitive one (cf. Schilder, 1924).

Let us now consider more closely the relation of the function of thinking, this foremost representative of the internalization process, to the tasks of adaptation, synthesis, and differentiation. In this connection we will have to disregard much that we know about thinking—for instance, its being energized by desexualized libido, its conjectured relation to the death instinct, its role as helper (rationalization) or opponent of the id, its dependence on the cathectic conditions, its facilitation or inhibition by the superego and by drive- and affect-processes, and so on. We expect the psychoanalysis of psychoses to help us bridge the gap between all these factors and those which will be considered here.

Freud states that the ego, by the interpolation of thought processes, achieves a delay of motor discharge. This process is part of an already discussed general evolution, namely, that the more differentiated an organism is, the more independent from the immediate environmental stimulation it becomes. Freud described thinking also as experimental action using small quantities of energy, and thereby elucidated both its biological function and its relation to action. It appears that in higher organisms, trial activity is increasingly displaced into the interior of the organism, and no longer appears in the form of motor action directed toward the external world. With this advance in evolution, human intelligence has reached that high point at which it affords man, whose somatic equipment is certainly in no way outstanding, his superiority over his environment.

Intelligence involves an enormous extension and differentiation of reaction possibilities, and subjects the reactions to its selection and control. Causal thinking (in relation to perception of space and time), the creation and use of means-end relations, and particularly the turning of thinking back upon the self, liberate the individual from being compelled to react to the immediate stimulus. The intellect understands and invents, and perhaps its function is even more to pose than to solve problems (Delacroix, 1936); it decides whether the individual will accept an event as it is, or will change it by his intervention (alloplastic adaptation); it seeks to control and steer the repetitive character of instincts and instinctual drives; it creates derivative needs, it turns means into ends and ends into means. Here we cannot always separate the various functions of the intellect (understanding, judgment, reasoning, etc.), though later on we will have something to say about this; nor can we discuss their development, their relation to perception (as in reality testing), to language, and so on.

Clearly, this whole broad area of functions pertains to the ego. I would hesitate, however, to equate it—as some do—with the ego. Intelligence has various definitions. According to W. Stern, it is "the general ability to meet new demands by purposive use of thought," and other authors, too, stress its biological function and adaptive character. Nevertheless, it would be a crude mistake to assume that a person's adaptability is proportionate to his intelligence (cf. Hermann

[1920], who has made many valuable contributions to the psychoanalytic theory of thought processes). Others have maintained that such biological considerations do not explain the nature of intelligence but only the use to which it is put. This view, in turn, was countered by the argument—see Claparède (1924), for instance—that the investigation of function may enrich our understanding of structure. Psychoanalysis has used this argument freely in its own field and thus—to my mind—must adopt it here too. Moreover, we are not concerned here with the phylogenetic problem—whether or not intelligence arose from adaptation—but with the fact that, once it exists, it serves adaptation. In any case, the emergence of intelligence is a decisive step in the development of purposive behavior. The stages of this development, says K. Bühler (1930), are instinct, habit, and intelligence. Even our sketchy presentation shows that intelligence performs, in part, tasks which at earlier stages were accomplished by other means, and, in part, introduces new functions. Such an articulation of behavior-forms into stages does not imply sharp dividing lines: even instinctual actions show adaptive changes and are not absolutely rigid. McDougall (1933) actually maintains that all behavior and all mental processes are both instinctual and intelligent. However, the greater plasticity of intelligence and its superiority in mastering new situations remains a fact—despite some possible reservations.

Certain schools of philosophy also attribute an important role to the biological function of thought and to its adaptation-facilitating relation to action, but their view of the relationship between "true" knowledge and its biological value is different from the one presented here. Pragmatism, for instance, does not take it for granted that agreement with reality is the criterion of the validity of certain propositions and that valid thought is the basis for survival-furthering actions, but—in a sense—holds the reverse: "man, when he follows recognized truth in his action, is successful because originally that 'truth' originated in the success of his action" says Simmel (1922) in one of his early studies. Thus he derives true and false—and the concept of truth in general—from the adaptive function of thought. This view certainly poses a problem for biological epistemology, but is only peripheral to our problems, to which we now return.

The functions of intelligence appear, as a rule, in a different light in the course of psychoanalysis than in this attempt to isolate them. In general we have no reason to separate intelligence from the network of relationships of the individual's life. We regard both typical and individual vicissitudes of instinctual drives as potentials for and limits of knowledge; we see intellectual achievements as both tools of conflict solving and of rationalizing, and consider them in relation to the demands of the external world and the superego and, of course, in their interaction with other ego functions. The analysis of inhibitions, neuroses, and particularly psychoses, has made us familiar with all degrees of disorder in the various functions of intelligence; and though the severe degrees occur only in psychoses, the milder, mostly temporary and reversible, forms are frequent in other mental illnesses. Each of the functions mentioned may be disturbed: selective control, time perspective, reality testing, objectivation, abstraction, ability to delay (Stärcke, 1935), and so on. A specific failure of adaptation corresponds to the disturbance of each of these functions.

Permit me a digression on the nature of thinking *in the psychoanalytic situation,* in which the predominant object of thought is the subject himself. Since the subject is always the means of action, even when he becomes the object of action, thinking renders basically the same service in the psychoanalytic situation as it does when it is directed to the external world. Psychoanalytic work shows that insight into one's own behavior depends on the assimilation of unconscious tendencies (of both ego and id). Nunberg (1937) has convincingly shown that the synthetic function of the ego directs these assimilation processes. Defenses (typically) not only keep thoughts, images, and instinctual drives out of consciousness, but also prevent their assimilation by means of thinking. When defensive processes break down, the mental elements defended against and certain connections of these elements become amenable to recollection and reconstruction. Interpretations not only help to regain the buried material, but must also establish correct causal relations, that is, the causes, range of influence, and effectiveness of these experiences in relation to other elements. I stress this here because the theoretical study of interpretation is often limited to those instances which are concerned with emerging memories or corresponding reconstructions. But even more important for the *theory of interpretation* are those instances in which the causal connections of elements, and the criteria for these connections, are established. We cannot assume that the ways in which children connect their experiences, and which later become conscious in the course of psychoanalysis, could satisfy the requirements of the mature ego, not to speak of the requirements of a judgment which has been sharpened by psychoanalytic means of thinking. This holds quite generally, and not just for the defense by isolation. The mere reproduction of memories in psychoanalysis can, therefore, only partly correct the lack of connection or the incorrect connection of elements.[1] An additional process

[1] [For a more detailed discussion, see "Technical Implications of Ego Psychology." *Psa. Quart.*, 20:31-43, 1951.]

comes into play here which may justly be described as a scientific process. It discovers (and does not rediscover), according to the general rules of scientific thinking, the correct relationships of the elements to each other. Here the theory of interpretation touches on the theory of mental connections and particularly on the distinction between meaning connections[2] and causal connections (compare Hartmann, 1927). Clearly, I do not concur with the often-voiced idea that the unconscious basically "knows it all" and that the task is merely to make this knowledge conscious by lifting the defense.

The infantile amnesias and peoples' forgetting the experiences of their psychoanalysis, once it is completed, amply demonstrate that healthy people too tend to conceal their mental life from themselves. We know that this may, but need not, become a source of disturbance. Self-deception may be due to the malfunction of self-perception or of thinking. In general we use the term self-deception only when the self has become the object of the intention to know, but not when it is simply taken for granted as the experiencing subject. There are typical as well as individual self-deceptions. Every instance of self-deception is accompanied by a misjudgment of the external world also. Psychoanalysis has systematized and can remedy these self-deceptions. Indeed, a great part of psychoanalysis can be described as a theory of self-deceptions and of misjudgments of the external world. In the course of the psychoanalytic process one learns to face one's own mental contents as objects of experience and thought and to see them as parts of a causal network. Thus, psychoanalysis is the highest development of thinking directed toward the inner life, in that it revises and regulates adaptation and

[2] ["Meaning connections" translates *verständliche Zusammenhänge*, in the sense of Dilthey's, Jaspers', and Spranger's *"verstehende Psychologie."—Tr.*]

fitting together (with all the biologically significant consequences for the individual that this implies).

Now we are on the path which leads from the general relationships between thinking and adaptation to the problem of *rational action,* and we will pursue it for a while. My necessarily sketchy presentation will be particularly incomplete in the face of the welter of problems encountered here.[3] In psychoanalysis we often speak about rational behavior: as a contrast to neurotic behavior, as a measuring rod of normality, as a goal of therapeutic efforts, as a guide in education, etc. Since we use adapted behavior too as the same kind of goal and measuring rod, its relation to rational action becomes important for us.

We have just spoken about the biological function of thinking, and we take it for granted that it is necessary to know, to assimilate, and to purposively influence reality. We do not share the malaise of our time, characterized by the fear that a surfeit of intelligence and knowledge will impoverish and denaturalize man's relationships to the world. To us this is a self-deception: no period in history has had a detrimental excess of knowledge or intelligence. We have no traffic with those who bemoan the mind as the "adversary of the soul" (Klages, 1929). The development of civilization has always been accompanied by an orchestra of voices expressing the fear that life might suffer from an overgrowth of intelligence, and in our own time it is particularly aggressive.

I make these remarks to forestall a misunderstanding of the discussion of the relation between rational action, adaptation, and synthesis, which follows here. We must admit that knowl-

[3] [For a more detailed treatment see "On Rational and Irrational Action." *Psychoanalysis and the Social Sciences,* 1:359-392. New York: International Universities Press, 1947.]

edge, when considered in the biological context of the adaptation problem, cannot be a goal in and of itself. Knowledge of reality must be subordinated to adaptation to reality, just as we subordinated adaptation to fitting together. Knowledge of reality cannot simply be equated with adaptation to reality; their relation has to be examined. It does not follow from the above-discussed relationships between thinking and environment that maximal rationality is also optimal adaptation and fitting together. When we say that a thought or a system of thoughts is "reality syntonic," we may have one of two different meanings in mind: first, that the theoretical content of these thoughts is true (that is, corresponds to actuality); second, that the translation of these thoughts into social action leads to adapted behavior. Clearly, the second meaning has the greater and more immediate biological significance. Thus, we ought not to judge whether or not an action is reality syntonic solely by the criterion that it is based on a good understanding of reality. Such a narrow view of the term "reality syntonic" would underestimate the central and special role of action and overestimate the importance of understanding. An action based on good understanding may have social consequences which by no means "further survival." There are countless economic and social examples of this. Advances of science—particularly in areas related to problems of personality—often result first in a disorientation which takes time to overcome. The fate of truths discovered prematurely, so to speak, is familiar to us all; they fare like prematurely given sexual explanations (see Freud, 1937). But while even these forgotten explanations may have a positive effect on individual adaptation, their historical counterpart has often had a less benign aspect. Here we might even speak of an antithesis between the adaptation of the individual and of the species.

Knowledge is bound to existence and place. Laforgue (1937) speaks of a "relativity of reality," meaning not only the actual dependence of individual and collective thinking upon ego development, but also the biological purposiveness of this coordination. In turn, however, if we regard the various thought-forms and world-views as consecutive steps in a process of adaptation, then we already attribute a certain "objectivity" to that reality to which individuals and peoples make their adaptations.

The term "rational" has many meanings, but we will discuss only those aspects of rational action which are directly relevant to our problem. Rational action has goals and means. Here we are particularly interested in those two types of action which Max Weber (1921) has distinguished as "goal-rational" and "value-rational." According to Weber, "a man's action is goal-rational if he considers the goals, the means and the side effects, and weighs rationally means against goals, goals against side effects, and also various possible goals against each other." If a man acts upon ethical, aesthetic, religious convictions, disregarding foreseeable consequences, then his action is purely value-rational: "Value-rational action (in our terms) is always action in accord with 'commandments' or 'demands,' which the actor believes he must follow." Weber's distinction is obviously analogous to the familiar one between action in the service of the ego and action in the service of the superego. But, let us add, this is not an absolute contrast: the ego may take up and sanction the superego's demands.

The goals of action are not rational in the usual sense unless they are partial goals in a broader means-goal complex. That is, only the choice of appropriate means to a given goal may be called rational. This fact is often overlooked, for instance, when the perspective is narrowed to ego interests, and thus what might be called a rational egotism is unquestioningly accepted as the basic human attitude; or, more generally, whenever any goal is "taken for granted" and thus its goal-character is lost sight of. We, on the contrary, stress the complexity of human needs and demands, and the broad range of goals which must be accepted as normal. Thus in what we would call rational behavior the goals—these orienting- and switching-points of action—are accepted as givens and the question is solely, what are the appropriate means of reaching them. When we speak of "sensible goals," we mean by "sensible" something quite different from what we here call "rational." If we were to pursue this train of thought, it would lead us to the problem of values. What concerns us here, however, is that while rational action, thus defined, certainly can serve within limits as a measuring rod, it obviously says very little about a person's general mental condition since it judges action only in terms of means-goals relationships.

We will also have to admit that the realm of strictly rational action is rather narrower than some of us would expect: we direct our actions by anticipating sequences of events, but in crucial areas of life only extremely rarely can we prognosticate with scientific certainty. Indeed, science often cannot tell us even what "the best technical means" to a goal are. In the meanwhile, action—at least in part—remains a matter of irrational decision; that is to say, even if we entirely disregard affective action, man is led not only by his rational motives, but also by habits, handed-down principles, self-evident propositions rooted in traditions, and the like. In spite of the great biological significance we ascribe to intelligence, we cannot deny that this other avenue is often just as successful. Laforgue's (1937) volume contains similar considerations showing that in the individual's adaptive achievements the role of the highly differentiated rational functions is neither general nor absolute.

The failure to recognize the limited role of intelligence in the total personality has occasionally led to a description of the totally rational man (in the just-defined and narrow sense) as the ideal, the paragon of health. This ideal is reminiscent of those caricatured conceptions of mental health which we encounter in our patients in the course of analysis. Since all those relatively stable forms of reaction which we call character qualities involve irrational elements—quite apart from the goals-means decisions they may imply—this ideal of the rational man is that of "a man without qualities" (if I may use the title of a well-known novel [Musil, 1930, 1932] in a different sense). Experience shows that the healthy and the analyzed man are quite unlike this "ideal." If we keep in mind what we said above about synthesis and rank order, we arrive at a very different picture: the optimal role of goal-means thinking in adaptation is decided by the maturity, the strength, and the structure of the ego.

Why then is this picture so distorted? Because in it a particular ability has taken the place of all other mental functions. The picture becomes much more human if we think of intelligence as *organizing* rather than taking the place of all other functions. At a certain level of development intelligence becomes aware of its own role as one function among others, sees its own activity in correct perspective among the other mental tendencies (and thereby overcomes the rationalistic prejudice which confuses the value it attributes to rational behavior with the actual effectiveness of rational behavior). Only after this broadening of awareness has been put at the disposal of action does intelligence serve the highest synthetic and differentiating functions of the ego. However, this form of synthesis is not conceptually identical with what is usually called "rational." This inclusion of other mental functions in the ego's plan of thought and action is an instance of its general anticipatory function, which involves knowledge both of man's relations to his environment and of his inner life. Not before psychoanalysis was the functioning of intelligence *in pure form* on this level possible, and we may say that the evolution of intelligence created in the form of psychoanalysis for the first time the means to do justice to this task. The prepsychoanalytic approaches to "rationality" had the primary (biological and social) shortcoming that they took into account only the conscious ego interests. "Rationalizations" in this sense—which is different from the psychoanalytic meaning of this term—must be, however, in several respects less adequate than the nonrational, "canalized" achievements of adaptation, which up to a point guarantee an equilibrium of the *whole person*. The history of our times offers many examples to substantiate this relationship. Actually, however, psychoanalysis does make possible a synthesis and a further development of adaptation-forms, though I cannot discuss here the extent to which society is or is not prepared to use this instrument.

The functioning of intelligence on this level may have two kinds of effects: it may lead to a better mastery of the environment (e.g., by taking into account the nature of other people, which involves an achievement in objectivation) and, what is particularly important, to a better control of one's own person. Historical development has brought now one and now the other of these to the fore as goals. At present many will agree that the second of these tasks has been neglected for too long. Karl Mannheim (1935) has investigated the mutual influences of the rationality of the social structure and the rationality of the individual's actions: his excellent book deserves the psychoanalyst's attention. He gives a masterly demonstration that industrialization on the one hand leads to increased "rationalization," and, on the other, through "massification," to all the irrationality implicit in mass psychology. It may be surmised that the emergence of psychoanalysis at this very point in history is connected with these developments, but here we cannot pursue these connections further. Apparently at certain points in history the ego can no longer cope with its environment, particularly not with that which it itself has created: the means and goals of life lose their orderly relation, and the ego then attempts to fulfill its organizing function by increasing its insight into the inner world. When is this condition an expression of a collective ego weakness and when is it due to an above-average environmental burden on the ego, are questions which we will bypass here. R. Waelder (1934a) has suggested that the alloplastic advance of our civilization has been so great that it must now be balanced by autoplastic changes, and psychoanalysis can contribute to effecting these changes which should adapt man to his new environment.

Our considerations have forced us to broaden the concept of "rationality," so that it becomes equivalent to the organizing function. This broader concept of rational behavior is a much better measuring rod of biologically and socially purposive behavior than the narrower concept we discussed first. I believe that Freud's famous proposition, "Where id was, there shall ego be" has often been misunderstood. It does not mean that there ever has been, or could be, a man who is purely rational; it implies only a cultural-historical tendency and a therapeutic goal. There is no danger that the id could ever be "dried up," nor that all the ego functions could be reduced to intellectual functions. In speaking of a "primacy of intelligence" we mean a "primacy of the regulation by intelligence," implying that regulation by intelligence takes the first place among the ego's regulatory factors, but not that all other mental functions can or should be replaced by it.

Freud (1932), after having expressed his hope that eventually intelligence would come to rule man's mental life, proceeded: "The very nature of reason is a guarantee that it would not fail to concede to human emotions and to all that is determined by them, the position to which they are entitled" (p. 234). Freud used the terms reason, intelligence, scientific spirit, as synonyms in this context. But perhaps we may pre-empt the term *reason*, in the sense Freud uses it here, for the organizing function we have been discussing to distinguish it from "comprehension of meaning," from causal thinking, etc.

It is crucial for the ego that it can use rational regulations, while it simultaneously takes into account the irrationality of other mental achievements. The rational plan must include the irrational as a fact. (Though here we are opposing the rational and the irrational, we are aware that this antithesis is relative.) Anthropomorphic and irrational thought can be fruitful even in the realm of scientific thinking; conversely, the need for rationality can be a symptom or a defense, etc., in pathological cases. (This—as is well known—can also be the case with a forced turning toward reality.) Thus we arrive at the insight that the tendency of psychoanalysis to enlighten must of necessity relativize the rationalistic doctrine of enlightenment. Even cursory reflection will show that the foundations of psychoanalysis as a therapeutic procedure indeed imply this relationship between regard for the rational and regard for the irrational elements.

A theory which takes one aspect of rationality and relativizes it in relation to the irrational, in order to attribute to another aspect of it the dominant role in mental life, implies two major dangers: on the one hand, the rationality of knowing may lead to a disregard of the significance of the irrational, and also to a failure to recognize the irrationality of the goals; on the other, reason may capitulate to irrationality. The latter is, in and of itself, the greater danger, though not for the psychoanalyst. The significance of rationality in various systems of *Weltanschauung* is relevant, but will not be discussed here: I have dwelt on it at length elsewhere (1933).

To return to our original problem: knowledge goes a long way in serving reality adaptation, but it does not go all the way; the more knowledge includes insight into its own function in the total personality structure and in environmental relations, the more it can serve adaptation. A concept akin to the "superordinate organizing function of intelligence," at which we have arrived here on psychoanalytic grounds, is apparently central in present-day sociological thinking also. I refer primarily to Karl Mannheim's book which I have recommended to your attention (cf. his comments on "interdependence-thinking").

6.

Some Integrative Functions of the Ego

We now return to the discussion of the ego's regulative principles, which we began with our description of thinking and rational action. At this point we should be able to say something about those regulating factors which are connected with the ego interests[1] and the will. However, psychoanalysis, concerned as it is with the regulation by the instinctual drives and thinking, has lost sight of the regulation by the will. Moreover, it was more important to psychoanalysis to view instinctual drive- and will-processes in the context of individual development, which connects them, rather than to differentiate them from each other. We know much about the dependence of the will on the needs, but little about its independent, specific psychological significance, though we recognize that it is steered by the external world more than the instinctual drives are. It may be surmised (Federn has on occasion made this point) that the psychology of will-

---

[1] [For a more detailed treatment of ego interests, see "Comments on the Psychoanalytic Theory of the Ego." *The Psychoanalytic Study of the Child,* 5:74-96. New York: International Universities Press, 1950; and "On Rational and Irrational Action." *Psychoanalysis and the Social Sciences,* 1:359-392. New York: International Universities Press, 1947.]

processes is destined to play a role in the psychoanalytic ego psychology of the future.

The full range of synthetic factors is not yet known: some of them belong to the superego, most of them to the ego, and some of these belong partly to the conflict-free regulative functions of the ego. We understand some of the unconscious synthetic factors; but we know very little of the preconscious and conscious ones. The hierarchies of values certainly belong in this context and fulfill a role similar to that which logic, the number series, etc., play in rational thinking, in that they can coordinate tasks and means of solution. (Their other role, which may result from an oversevere superego, is so familiar that it need not be discussed here.) We should not underestimate the importance of these value hierarchies among those socially determined hierarchies which the child must come to terms with, and by accepting which he becomes a part of "a world in which men have put a law over themselves," says S. Bornstein-Windholz (1937) in an excellent paper. The child, by accepting these values, may find an appropriate way to cope with his libidinal and aggressive impulses, and his acceptance thus may amount to a synthetic achievement. But, of course, not all elements of the social value hierarchy will lend themselves equally to this use. The superindividual nature of such value systems and ideals facilitates cooperation with other people and thus adaptation also. Social value-systems are just like any other conventions (in the broadest sense of the word): though they often hinder adaptation, under certain conditions they can also facilitate it. Freud (1921), when he discusses the social significance of ideal-formation, deals with the crystallization of some of those goals which determine the direction of rational action. (Here again Max Weber's distinction between goal-rational and value-rational action is relevant.) In this context "goal" need not have a final, that is, absolute connotation. Goals, says Dewey (1922), are in general means "to unify and to liberate present, contradictory, confused habits and drives"; his terminology is, of course, different from ours. This form of adaptation, like any other, is suitable only in average expectable situations. The social norms which the child adopts only partly coincide with the rewards and punishments he will actually receive from society in later life. Nevertheless, these value hierarchies may serve as switching-stations or crystallization points of human behavior: we have seen that action presupposes not only rational regulation but also goals set by the hierarchies of values. The significance of such value hierarchies formed in the individual varies according to the structure of the society in which they arise, for instance, according to whether the ethics realized in a society tend to be more of a narcissistic or more of a compulsion-neurotic type, etc. Some such hierarchies of values may be directly hostile, others neutral to society, and some will contain social factors of the highest significance, as, for example, the valuation of the love for fellow men. Freud (1926a) commented: "Given our drive dispositions and our environment, the love for fellow men must be considered just as indispensable for the survival of mankind as is technology." Thus the adoption of ethical value hierarchies may fulfill a task of synthesis and it may, but need not, be useful for individual adaptation. We will be more impressed with the usefulness of these value hierarchies if we take into account their role in the maintenance of society (or certain kinds of society). I have briefly mentioned and will not discuss further the difficult question whether we fare better if our concept of adaptation includes the survival of the individual only or that of the species as well. I want to stress here again that for simplicity's sake I have neglected, and will continue to neglect, just those connections which are usually of the greatest interest to us: how the tendency to build such "hierarchies of values" develops, what reaction formations play a role in this development, what anxieties are mastered by it, and what the sources of these anxieties are. We cannot dwell on these matters here.

We are familiar with the relationship between the arts and magic action. The artistic form retains something of its magic origins; but it is just here that it is better not to speak of a separation of form and content: when we use the term "magic" in the strict sense, then form is also content. A change of function takes place in the course of the development of art: Kris (1934) has shown that what began as magic effect becomes artistic value. Here evolution takes two courses: one leads to rational (and ultimately to scientific) representation, the other to artistic representation. The two clearest end products of this evolution are the conceptual language of science, which is a purely rational representation, and the language of poetry. Art is certainly not a mere archaic residue. Apparently, just because of their origin, the once magic images provide varied possibilities for synthetic solutions. Over and above the question of their suitability for need gratification, these magic images retain their potency as orienting-points, even on a higher level of development. Here again we have a multiple layering like that which I have demonstrated in thinking. The process of artistic creation is the prototype of synthetic solution, and (besides its secondary relation to social reality, described by Freud, 1917) this is the most important difference between it and "fantasying." Such a tendency toward "order" is inherent in every work of art, even when its content or intent represents "disorder." This is, then, another case of "regressive adaptation": a mental achievement (whose roots are archaic) gains a new significance both for synthesis and in relation to the external world, precisely because of the detour through the archaic. We have disregarded here the relation of art to the instinctual drives and have considered only its role in the framework of (nonrational) ego functions. Naturally, beauty also gives pleasure and is dependent on instinctual drives; moreover, the work of art yields both a primary, and (through its synthetic achievement) a secondary pleasure. Freud's work on wit might open the way to the understanding of the economy of these effects; however, art has in addition that normative, ordering element which I have just discussed, and even then this characterization of the psychological meaning of art and works of art is very incomplete. Kris's studies of the last few years contain possible points of departure for bridging the gap between psychoanalytic ego psychology and aesthetics. One more factor should be mentioned here which is also a prototype (or representative) of an important ego function of great biological value: it is the increased mobility of the ego in artistic activity and artistic enjoyment, which may be related to the ego's mobility in play and in the comic. This "mobility" is, to begin with, a freedom from the regulation by the external world; since, however, it also affords access to the inner world, it can have autoplastic effects also. At this point there are several connections between the synthetic function of the ego (and perhaps even the more primitive "fitting together"), and the problem of gestalt (spatial, temporal, thought- and action-gestalt, etc.).

Though all these comments are tentative and, of course, very incomplete, I cannot close this section without a reference to the psychological significance of religions. Religions are (among other things) objectivations of a value scale. We are familiar with Freud's genetic derivation from a single source of the elements which are integrated in religious systems, namely their attempts at consolation, at explanation of the unknown, and at creating a system of ethical imperatives. The continued influence on the human mind and the synthetic achievement of religions rest on their integrative imagery and on their being tradition-saturated, socially unifying wholes which are fed by the contributions of all the three mental institutions, and provide a pattern, accessible to many people, for satisfying the demands of all these three institutions (cf. also Leuba, 1937). Religions are the most obvious attempt to cope both with these mental institutions and with social adaptation (through forming communities) by means of synthesis.

7.

Implications for the Concepts of Health and Education

THE ISSUES of adaptation, synthesis, rank order, and rational action lead us to the question of the possible criteria for *the concept of mental health*.[1] The solution is simple whenever freedom from symptoms and health can be equated. If we add the factor of enduring freedom from symptoms and resistance to disruptions, we are still in a realm which is easily dealt with empirically, though not prognostically. But beyond the range where these criteria can be applied, it is very hard to give a scientific definition of mental health, or to define the state to which we want to lead our patients by the means of psychoanalysis. All the contexts in which we have here encountered the concept of health give us hints, but none—and not even all of them together—yield a sufficiently broad, flexible, and unequivocal definition of it. Moreover, health is, in part, a very individual matter. Finally, the commonly used criteria of health are obviously colored by *Weltanschauung*, by "health-morality," by social and political goals. In the analysis of our patients we have become familiar with the psychological background for the various concep-

[1] [For a more detailed treatment, see "Psychoanalysis and the Concept of Health." *Int. J. Psa.*, 20:308-321, 1939.]

tions of health. I believe, therefore, that for the time being, we will have to forego the formulation of a definitive and general theoretical concept of health, lest we unwittingly base the evaluation of our experience and the formation of the concept on our own subjective goals. Still another consideration should caution us against making hasty pronouncements about the attributes of "ideal" health (a concept formed mainly as an antithesis of neurosis): the recurrent observation that the very mechanisms which lead to obvious pathology can, under different conditions, serve adaptive reactions, and that the outcome often depends on a quantitative rather than a structural factor. A concept of health which is conceived solely as the negative of neurosis and disregards the state of the conflict-free sphere is too narrow, if only because without taking this sphere into account, the concepts of ego strength, rank order, and equilibrium cannot be satisfactorily delineated. Another reason why some theoretical concepts of health are too narrow is that they usually underestimate both the great variety of personality types which must, practically speaking, be considered healthy and the many personality types which are socially necessary. Thus at present we must limit our theory to the exploration of the concrete relationships of mental functions to adaptive and synthetic processes and achievements. But all this does not alter our practice, does not change the aims of psychoanalytic therapy (which, from the vantage point of a future theoretical concept of health, are tentative aims): to help men achieve a better functioning synthesis and relation to the environment. I will limit myself to these few remarks, since I have spoken about these issues in greater detail last March.

We encounter similar difficulties when we attempt to derive theoretically the goal of education from the factors of adaptation, synthesis, etc. What underlies this derivation is analogous to what underlies the theoretical concept of health; but here we already know that the goal of education cannot be satisfactorily defined in terms of the concept of neurosis-prevention alone. From the general biological point of view the process of education undoubtedly aims primarily at the adaptation and particularly the socialization of the child. But education actually goes beyond these aims and also instills certain ideals, which are usually, at least in part, fixed by tradition, but which may also become the means to change society. The adoption of prescribed forms and goals of behavior can, and certainly often does, facilitate adaptation, but it can also obstruct it. We may perhaps distinguish three elements in all forms of education: the adaptation to the given environment; the preparation for an anticipated future environment; and the molding of goals according to the educating generation's ideals, in which the past, as well as the present and future, usually has a voice too. Of course, rational behavior, dominance of the regulation by intelligence, and the like, can also be an educational ideal. But their rational character notwithstanding, once they are set up as such an ideal, then—just like any other educational ideal—they are the expression of a nonrational value system and are not what we would call rational. I merely touch on this here, since I have discussed it in detail elsewhere (1933). Freud (1927) has asked why it is that religious systems unite cosmogony and ethical norms (here we may disregard the third element of religion, "consolation"). He answers in genetic terms, that both originate in the child's relation to the father. This urge to derive elements of knowledge and normative elements from each other and to trace them to a common matrix, which we find in religions, is, however, also observable outside of them (for example, in many metaphysical systems) and in nonreligious people. Apparently the majority of men cannot tolerate the idea that not even from safe, tested knowledge can we logically deduce a reason for the "thou shalt." This majority clings to the illusion that knowledge should provide the goals of action, and thus they transfer the "dignity" of knowledge to those goals for the realization of which this knowledge is used, as though ethical or educational goals could be proved "true" by applying "true" knowledge to achieve them. But these two usages of "true" have different meanings: one means agreement with an accepted system of values, the other means agreement with reality. Repeated attempts have been made—primarily in the last decades of the past century and this time presumably in the name of science—to fulfill this urge and to reduce the "thou shalt" to an "is" by introducing concepts like "biological value." But these still left the matter in the realm of value hierarchies. It is naturally true—and I have discussed this elsewhere (1928)—that the deepening of a man's knowledge may change his valuations. But the crucial point which that illusion tries to deny remains unchanged: the "validity" of the knowledge which codetermines an act of valuation has nothing to do with the "validity" of that valuation. Knowledge, however, can help us to recognize that what is "really" our own hierarchy of values—that is, the actual structure and goals of our value-rational actions—does not coincide with the value-system which we had consciously considered our own. Psychoanalysis frequently effects such changes: for instance, it may turn up contradictory valuations, it may show that partial valuations disagree with general ones, and it may disprove an assumed "means-end relation" between two values—by virtue of which one of these is secondarily derived from the other which is a primary value. Moreover, new attitudes toward the self and the environment, acquired in the course of psychoanalysis, may find their expression in new acts of valuation, and so on. But we cannot concur with the view that values can be *derived* from psychoanalytic knowledge, or with the view that the actual changes in valuation which result from analysis can lead to a really uniform hierarchy of values, common to all analyzed people—though of course certain common elements are demonstrable in the value hierarchies of those people who have had similar experiences or who, in their analyses, have had to correct similar self-deceptions. It is certain that, because of a relativistic attitude, one may tend to erroneously underestimate the commonalities between the actually existing ethical and other hierarchies of values. The elements common to all men in coming to terms with the environment, in the infantile situation, in superego formation, etc., result, of course, in common elements of value systems but not in a common value system, as a glance at history readily shows. The belief that the level of rationality attained by analyzed men, and the analyzed person's increased knowledge of his own developmental history, should lead to a hierarchy of values accepted by all analyzed people, seems to me to be just as unfounded as the belief that there should be no individual differences in analyzed peoples' other behavior.

A "natural" value hierarchy, valid for all men, does not exist. "Natural," in this context, is a screen for a hidden valuation, and is used to make subjective goals appear as objective knowledge. I found an impressive example of this in Seneca. Since he condemns sensuality but favors natural life, he proceeds to prove that sensuality must be basically unnatural. The same applies to so-called "natural" education. One of the reasons why "normal" development is hard to delineate is the fact that in it biological and social factors shade into each other; obviously, in man there can be no such thing as undisturbed development (in the sense of one uninfluenced by social environment). Consequently, passive behavior in educators is just as much an "intervention" as active behavior, nonenlightenment just as much as enlightenment, noninterpretation just as much as interpretation, nonprohibition just as much as prohibition, and so on. In short, the development and education of the child is often called natural when it is considered "right," that is, when it is positively valued.

What I have said about the conflict-free sphere, ego strength, adaptation, fitting together, rank order of ego functions, ordering principles in the ego, and so on, is also a preparation for the ego aspect of a future, more adequate, concept of adaptation and health.

8.

Preconscious Automatisms

WE HAVE already touched on the problem of *action* (though so far I have discussed only rational action) in terms of its motivation. Now we shall take a closer look at it, though I can select from the total problem only fragments of a few themes which seem important for our conception of ego structure and of the "healthy" ego. An investigation such as this one, which uses man's relation to his environment as its point of departure, should perhaps focus on action. In the study of intrapsychic conflict, action can be temporarily bracketed, so to speak, but as soon as we turn to the study of adaptation processes, it immediately takes the center of the stage. Freud has shown that one of the manifestations of the transition from the pleasure principle to the reality principle is the development of action from a mere motor discharge. A genetic psychology of action would be equally important for the theories of ego development, intention, and object relations.

In the course of psychoanalysis we encounter many situations in which it is important for us to know the extent to which our patients' actions are realistic. Actually, very often we cannot adequately determine the *coefficient of realism*—to coin a phrase. When we apply psychoanalytic thinking to sociological and ethnopsychological problems, this determination becomes even more difficult than it is in the analysis of individuals. The simplest example in an individual analysis is when we are to determine whether the dangerousness of an adversary is real or a projection of aggressive impulses. Similarly, when we apply psychoanalytic insights to other fields, our considerations always include judgments concerning the actual social structure, that is, concerning an extra-analytic independent factor. Furthermore, not only is it difficult to determine how realistic an action is, but the concept "realistic" is itself equivocal. We consider an action realistic, first of all, when it is realistic in its intention, that is, when its means are chosen according to its goals in the light of correctly appraised external (and internal) conditions. We call such actions "subjectively reality syntonic." We also consider realistic those actions which fit into the conditions of the external world so that they actually further the reality relations of the individual. We call these actions "objectively reality syntonic."[1] The questions which interest us here are these: to what extent is realistic regulation of action determined by intention and rational motivation and to what extent by the state of adaptation of the apparatuses used by the action; moreover, to what extent does an action motivationally or genetically involve irrational forces—that is, instinctual drives—and so on? I cannot pursue here further the problem of the reality-relationships which are involved in the psychology of action.

Actions always involve the body: they always imply an awareness of the subject's own body on some level of consciousness (cf. Schilder, 1924). The ego uses somatic apparatuses to execute actions. I will discuss first the motor apparatuses. In adults they are organized for certain achieve-

[1] [See also "On Rational and Irrational Action." *Psychoanalysis and the Social Sciences,* 1:359-392. New York: International Universities Press, 1947.]

ments. In well-established achievements they function automatically: the integration of the somatic systems involved in the action is automatized, and so is the integration of the individual mental acts involved in it. With increasing exercise of the action its intermediate steps disappear from consciousness. To explain this Kretschmer (1922) proposed a law of "formular abbreviation." The disorders of automatized actions, particularly those due to organic brain disease, give us important information about the function of the somatic apparatuses involved in action, while we learn about the function of the mental apparatuses involved from developmental psychology and from psychoanalysis (particularly of psychotics).

Not only motor behavior, but perception and thinking, too, show *automatization*. Exercise automatizes methods of problem-solving just as much as it does walking, speaking, or writing. (It is generally known, and well described by K. Groos [1903], that disturbances of automatized achievements reactivate flexible intelligence.) Observations of automatized functions, and of some other phenomena as well, warn us that the conception of a thoroughly flexible ego is an illusion; yet normally even well-established actions and methods of thinking are not completely rigid. Besides the adaptedness implicit in their use, automatized activities have a certain leeway (of varying latitude) for adaptation to the momentary situation.

We consider misleading, and will therefore reject, any theory which would reduce the complexity of human activities to a system of "habits" which are exercised or canalized to varying degrees. Such theories—propounded primarily in the United States and in a particularly extreme form by Dewey (1922)—completely overlook the personal element, the regulation of human actions by the ego. The arguments against this excessively monistic conception of mental life are obvious and have often been stated. Our concern here is only to indicate the place of automatisms within the superordinate mental structure. In doing so I will avoid the term "habit." Habits and automatisms are certainly in many ways related forms of behavior regulation. Habit is the broader, but the vaguer, of the two concepts. To say that we do something "as a habit" means that we always do it in certain situations, without being able to state its motivation or purpose. Of course a habit can, nevertheless, have a "meaning" which is not conscious. Habit formation can be initiated by a drive-demand or by a defense against a drive, or by both. The role of identifications and of other social relations is often clearly demonstrable in habits (cf. Bernfeld, 1930).

The place of these automatisms in the mental topography is the *preconscious*. In his *Wit and Its Relation to the Unconscious*, Freud (1905a) wrote: "These processes which take place in the preconscious and lack the attention-cathexis which is the prerequisite of consciousness are appropriately termed 'automatic.' "[2] It is certain, however, that not all the preconscious processes are automatic and that they also bring about extensive recombinations of elements. Janet (1930) frequently uses the term automatism, but his usage is ambiguous, since he subsumes under it a variety of processes including most of those which we consider unconscious in the strict sense, particularly the mechanisms of the unconscious. I cannot reconcile the concept of automatism—used here in the sense of a formular abbreviation, of apparatus formation —with our view of id functioning. Automatization in this sense surely presupposes cathectic conditions of a sort which we ascribe to the preconscious but not to the id. Though we

---

[2] [This passage appears on p. 791 of Brill's translation (Freud, 1905a), but here it is retranslated from the German.—*Tr*.]

might call the repetition compulsion an automatic process since it is relatively free from ego influence, and though we do speak of automatic anxiety in contrast to the anxiety signal, and so on, these usages differ from my use of the concept here, even though they may all prove, upon investigation, to be related (more about this further on). The use of a term is after all a matter of definition; the term "automatism" here is applied only to the somatic and preconscious ego apparatuses, and note that here again we encounter a problem which suggests that we should extend our psychological efforts to the study of the preconscious.

Compulsion neuroses, tics, catatonias, etc., have taught us something about pathological automatisms. Normal automatisms are frequently the predecessors of compulsion symptoms, and in compulsion neuroses we see how they develop into symptoms. Freud (1926b) describes how compulsion symptoms fasten onto "procedures (which later on become almost automatic) in connection with going to sleep, washing, dressing, and locomotion" (p. 67). It is also well known that sexualization of automatic functions plays a role in many neuroses. Landauer (1927) has demonstrated that compulsion neuroses may prevent de-automatization in order to guard against the becoming conscious of forbidden impulses and the mobilization of guilt feelings. He considers automatization—by which "the pleasure- and pain-experiencing ego is stifled"—to be the obverse of projection, by which the ego animistically vitalizes its environment, endowing it with a soul. Fenichel (1928) studied certain impairments of the ego's "control of motility," the dystonic automatic postures, and established their functional relation to anxiety, defense, and organ-libidinal processes. The role of automatic reactions, automatic defense processes, etc., in the genesis of the neurotic character which was described by W. Reich (1933), is also pertinent to this point, and so are his inferences concerning the technique of psychoanalysis.

Here we are not directly concerned with such pathological automatization processes, nor with automatisms as the starting points for pathological developments, nor even with the pertinent problems of technique. Alexander (1921, 1925) has set this problem into a broader context and I agree with him on many points; but even he treats automatization mainly as a flight from reality, as a regressive phenomenon. Our concern here is with the purposive achievements of these automatisms and with their important role in the scheme of adaptation processes. It cannot be a matter of "chance" that automatisms play so great a role among those functions which are either adaptive themselves, or are used by adaptation processes. It is obvious that automatization may have economic advantages, in saving attention cathexis in particular and simple cathexis of consciousness in general. In using automatisms we apply means which already exist, which we need not create anew at every occasion, and consequently the means-end relations in some areas are, so to speak, "not subject to argument." In the case of physiological automatisms, it is known that increased practice decreases their metabolic requirements. These apparatuses achieve what we expect of any apparatus: they facilitate the transformation and the saving of energy. The success of many complicated achievements in central mental regions depends on automatization. Here, as in most adaptation processes, we have a purposive provision for the average expectable range of tasks. It is possible that automatization functions as a stimulus barrier in the mental apparatus. It should be mentioned that no new automatisms are formed in old age, though the so-called "habits" play an important role.

Automatisms—like other mental phenomena previously

discussed—too may be said to be under the control of the external world, and under certain conditions, a formularly abbreviated behavior is a better guarantee of reality mastery than a new adaptation to every occasion. In this sense even achievements of great biological adaptation value, like flexible thinking and action, may disrupt adaptation by interfering with the automatized process at an unsuitable point or to an unsuitable degree. Automatization is a characteristic example of those relatively stable forms of adaptedness which are the lasting effects of adaptation processes. The sweeping assertion that one of the goals of psychoanalysis is to transform these automatisms into mobile ego-processes (that is, into processes which adapt anew at every occasion) does not do justice to the adaptation value of such preconscious automatic activities.

Ego rigidity is a well-known obstacle to adaptation. We must, however, amend this formulation since automatisms can also be superior forms of functioning. The misapprehension which we are trying to correct apparently has two sources: first of all, our conception of the ego functions is modeled too schematically on a single ego function (that is, the choice between alternatives); secondly, we neglect the adapted forms of behavior in favor of the processes of adaptation which are, of course, more conspicuous. Actually both flexibility and automatization are necessary to and characteristic of the ego; purposive achievements depend on some functions taking a flexible, others an automatized form, and still others combining these two forms in various proportions. The ego must also be able to encompass automatized functions in its adaptation processes. May I remind you that we have already encountered such an *inclusion of the antithesis* in an entirely different field: rational action must include irrational elements in its plan. Here again we are faced with the almost untouched problems of the structure formation within the ego and of the rank order of ego functions in terms of their biological purposiveness.

The automatisms are "musts" too (though this "must" is naturally only a special case of thoroughgoing psychological determinism). Not all automatisms can be altered immediately and without transition by a mere decision of will. These "musts" and those of compulsion symptoms are not, of course, experienced in the same way. However, the disturbances caused by interrupting automatisms and compulsion symptoms are similar; but so are those caused by interrupting ego-syntonic drive-actions: even the rationally justified interruption of sexual activity amounts to a disturbance and displeasure. We usually consider it pathognomonic if people find it difficult to make decisions, are not masters of their actions, or have no access to certain mental acts and areas over which most people do have command. In this context Waelder (1934b) prefers the terms "free" and "unfree"; and so does Goldstein (1939) in characterizing the behavior of the brain-injured. I avoid the term "free," since in the history of philosophy it has acquired so many connotations that it must inevitably lead to misunderstandings; however, the facts to which the term refers do stand and may even provide one of the criteria of health (among others) in certain instances. The interpretation of these facts, of course, is subject to argument. What I am implying here is that *the control by the conscious and the preconscious ego,* its degree and its scope, has a positive significance for health, although the "must" and the "inability-to-do-otherwise" are not always unequivocal criteria of pathology. Oversimplified theoretical conceptions of health disregard these empirical facts. Healthy people too obey "musts." They are not mollusks; they have "characteristics" and these are simply relatively stable reaction-forms which are not reconsidered at every occasion. Luther's, "Here I stand—I cannot do otherwise" is not pathological behavior.

The formulations referred to above imply first of all the commonplace that a person is healthy if his behavior is "adequate" in every situation; the problem, however, is to establish what in the given mental conditions—which are not subject to change at will—offers the best chance to achieve adequacy. Perhaps these formulations also imply that decisions must use means-end relations in an objectively correct fashion, that they must be rationally motivated. But we have already seen that "rational" is not to be used as a magic word, cannot stand above purposiveness, nor does it say anything about the tasks themselves, about what the ego can do and what the normal ego should be able to do. Logical insight is certainly only one of the regulatory factors. The automatisms put an additional obstacle in the way of arriving at a criterion of mental health: the normal ego must be *able* to control, but it must also be *able to must;* and this fact, far from vitiating it, is necessary for its health. Likewise, the normal ego must be able to suspend, temporarily, even its most essential functions. An example of this is the so-called "ego-loss" in intense sexual excitement, the pathological forms of which is familiar clinically as anxiety about this ego-loss in orgasm (cf., for instance, Fenichel, 1937a). We conclude that the normal ego is able to yield to musts. (Akin to this is the ego's abandoning itself to free associations in the course of psychoanalysis. In this case the ego-controlled suspension of certain ego functions has to be learned; it is known that children cannot do it.) We do not underestimate the "freely mobile function of the ego"—one of our best allies in our therapeutic work—by saying that the ego must not be equated with one of its functions,[3] in this case flexible thinking and action; that the healthy ego thinks and acts flexibly, but not exclusively so; furthermore, that in the healthy human being certain superordinate ego functions determine when the ego can make purposive use of automatisms; and finally that in the service of ego regulations even highly developed ego achievements must be temporarily suspended. This superordinate ego function apparently represents what might be called "central regulation" or perhaps "goal structure" (cf. pp. 67-72 concerning goals and means).

What is the relation of these automatisms to the pleasure principle and to the repetition compulsion? Apparently these relatively rigid apparatuses often perpetuate something that was once pleasurable, in that it mastered a task, or removed a disturbance, or the like. We have already stressed that formular abbreviation essentially favors reality relations. It is possible that the "principles"—as we conceive of them—only trigger the repetition of canalized actions and methods of thought (since they have been structuralized), but do not regulate their subsequent course. Since automatized processes are repetitive, one might think that they are somehow related to the repetition compulsion. This coordination would be even obvious, if we—like Alexander (1925)—called every repetition of previously successful mastery repetition compulsion. The implication of Freud's (1920) examples of the repetition compulsion, however, is different. According to Freud, the fixating factor of the repetition compulsion is beyond the pleasure principle, overrides the pleasure principle. The repetition of experiences, in the narrower sense, should per-

[3] [On partial ego concepts, see "Psychoanalysis and Developmental Psychology." *The Psychoanalytic Study of the Child*, 5:7-17. New York: International Universities Press, 1950; and "The Mutual Influences in the Development of Ego and Id." *The Psychoanalytic Study of the Child*, 7:9-30. New York: International Universities Press, 1952.]

haps also be distinguished from the repetition of methods of solution. There certainly are repetitions which follow the pleasure principle, and therefore we must not take every repetition for an expression of the repetition compulsion. There are fixations to gratification situations, as well as to traumata.

According to Nunberg (1937), direct observation of children shows that "it is the constant struggle between the retarding tendencies of the repetition compulsion and the hunger for new impressions that leads little by little to the mastering of reality. In the course of this process the repetition-compulsion gradually recedes into the background" (p. 171). But here we must distinguish between two kinds of "repetition": first, the small child's constant repetition of the same action and rearousal of the same situation; second, our present concern, the automatization of actions and thinking, as a result of which certain tasks are always mastered in the same or in a very similar way. These two may fuse in some behaviors but they may also appear separately and frequently do so. The first of these plays a prominent role in the studies of child psychologists and is the subject of an interesting psychoanalytic study by Spitz (1937), which shows that this type of repetition recedes around the sixth year, that it appears later only under certain conditions (rhythm, etc.), and that this recession is related to the passing of the Oedipus complex. We may assume that in these repetitions the repetition compulsion and the pleasure principle frequently interlock, as Freud demonstrated in children's play. One of the factors at work here is the familiar active repetition of passive experiences. Spitz leaves open the possibility of a relation to the repetition compulsion and stresses pleasure-gain and pain-avoidance (clinging to the familiar which does not threaten pain; and avoiding the new and threatening). The explanation of repetition as a saving in energy expenditure is apparently insufficient in many cases. Guernsey's well-known example, quoted by Spitz (1937), is typical: a child of eleven months stumbles in his bed and bangs his forehead hard; after a few minutes of loud crying he proceeds to bang his forehead several dozen times, for about half an hour. Ch. Bühler (1928) explains such instances as "exercise of function." From the biological point of view, that is, from the point of view of a possible adaptive significance, this explanation cannot be rejected; from the psychological point of view, however, we can and must add to it—as Waelder (1932) has shown—the explanation by the repetition compulsion.

The heuristic potential of psychological analysis in regard to this biological realm of adaptive functions and regulative principles I have discussed above in another context (pp. 34-35). Psychoanalysis has, certainly, no objections to K. Bühler's (1929) concept of "pleasure in functioning" (that is, pleasure inherent in activity whatever its goals and consequences, in contrast to gratification pleasure). Indeed, Freud took this form of pleasure-gain into account quite early (1905a): "When we do not use our psychic apparatus to secure indispensable gratifications, then we let it work so as to derive pleasure out of its own activity." But not even this concept of pleasure in functioning suffices to explain the repetition phenomena of childhood.

We have already made the point that the repetition phenomena in children, studied by Spitz, are brought about either by the repetition compulsion or by the pleasure principle (or both).[4] Automatisms, however, obviously differ from these repetitions and also from those Nunberg refers to, since they do not recede at the sixth year but, on the contrary,

[4] [My further elaboration of these thoughts is quoted by Edward Bibring in his paper on "The Conception of the Repetition Compulsion." *Psa. Quart.*, 12:486-519, 1943.]

continue to prevail (for example, in learning). Nor are these automatisms—being apparently more ego syntonic—later replaced by "boredom" as are the repetitions Spitz describes. The chronology of development contradicts any attempt to view automatization as a means of overcoming these other forms of repetition. I doubt if Freud's concept of the repetition compulsion, in its proper sense, is applicable to automatisms; but perhaps a "domesticated" form of repetition compulsion could be. Nunberg (1932) seems to have something like this in mind when he says that the repetition compulsion may be deprived of its independence and impetus by the synthetic forces of the ego. Actually, the repetition compulsion is the older form of regulation; it can overrule ego regulation, it can occasionally serve the same tendency as the ego regulation does, but under certain conditions the ego can put it to its own use. Hermann (1922) assumes that the repetition compulsion develops into "orderly repetition" ("ordinance"). In any case, we must realize that all these attempts to relate the automatisms to the repetition compulsion would imply that the repetition compulsion is—in the adult as well as in the child—an essential driving force of that function which leads to reality mastery through learning, and whose role—particularly in man—is central.

It is not improbable that the repetition compulsion has its share (besides the pleasure principle and the reality principle) in learning processes, but if so, then the reality-regulated ego tendencies (cf. French, 1937) must use the repetition compulsion's tendencies selectively. Therefore, I would prefer to speak of a partial interaction between the repetition compulsion and the ego-dependent activities of the mental apparatus, rather than of an "ego aspect of the repetition compulsion." It should also be remembered that (according to these considerations) this would be but *one* of the roots of mental automatisms. Freud introduced the repetition compulsion as a characteristic of the *instinctual drives* (cf. also Jones, 1936); our applying it here to a remote field naturally leaves many uncertainties.

9.

Ego Apparatuses. Autonomous Ego Development

WE RETURN once more to the problem of action. In action the ego uses both somatic and mental apparatuses. "Mental apparatus" is a particularly fitting description of the preconscious automatisms (and not only of those which pertain to action); however, since it implies structure and formedness, as all concepts of apparatuses do, it is hardly applicable to what is occasionally termed the automatic character of the id. Bleuler (1920), when he coined the term "occasional apparatus" to explain the process of "abreaction," had something analogous in mind; but we cannot dwell here on this special use of the concept. Schilder (1928) also uses the concept of apparatus frequently, and maintains that "function is facilitated by the very fact that the organism is a structure." Actions, therefore, always imply intentions, acts of will, motives, etc. on the one hand, and (mental and physical) apparatuses on the other. Thus far investigators have paid little attention to the role of these apparatuses in the possibility, direction, success, and development of action. However, if we take the conflict-free ego sphere into consideration and if we want to develop a general psychology of action, the study of these apparatuses becomes imperative, because otherwise all our statements about action include an unknown: the prediction of actions presupposes the knowledge of these apparatuses. Here again it may be objected that all these problems are outside the field of psychoanalysis. This is incorrect, however, if we seriously intend to develop the ego psychology begun by Freud, and if we also want to investigate those functions of the ego which cannot be derived from the instinctual drives. These functions belong to the realm which we term—with some obvious reservations—*autonomous ego-development*. (Here I will not discuss how disturbances in this realm can become independent factors in pathology; Nunberg, Schilder, and E. Bibring have made a start in this direction.) It is obvious that these apparatuses, somatic and mental, influence the development and the functions of the ego which uses them; we maintain that these apparatuses constitute one of the roots of the ego.[1] Schilder (1937) showed this very clearly when he demonstrated that a disorder of the central equilibrium apparatus may influence object-relations. An example of more general significance is the effect of language development on thinking. For us, it goes without saying that the apparatuses, both congenital and acquired, need a driving force in order to function; and that the psychology of action is inconceivable without the psychology of instinctual drives.

The individual does not acquire all the apparatuses which are put into the service of the ego in the course of development: perception, motility, intelligence, etc., rest on constitutional givens. These components of *"ego constitution"* deserve our attention just as much as the components of drive constitution. Naturally, the antithesis of ego (as a regulative factor) and ego apparatuses must not be equated with the

[1] [See also "Comments on the Psychoanalytic Theory of the Ego." *The Psychoanalytic Study of the Child*, 5:74-96. New York: International Universities Press, 1950.]

antithesis of environmentally determined and constitutional. The ego as a regulative agency too has constitutional roots. In the course of psychoanalysis, ego constitution (just like drive constitution) appears in its negative aspect, so to speak, that is, as a limit to the explanation of a behavior by environmental influences. But outside of psychoanalysis a great advance toward direct proof of the inheritance of mental characteristics has been made in the last twenty years: we now have, thanks primarily to research on twins,[2] tested knowledge independent of the previous arbitrary nativistic or empiricistic conceptions.

We know that many ego functions—though certainly not all, and some only in part—are molded on the patterns of instinctual drives. This is surely the case for "giving," "taking," etc., and partly also for the ego mechanisms of introjection and projection, but probably not for perception and motility. As I have discussed on another occasion (1927), perceptual processes cannot simply be considered projections (or introjections) in our sense. In some cases it will be advisable to assume that both the instinctual drive processes and the ego mechanisms arise from a common root prior to the differentiation of the ego and the id; though after they have structuralized, they may secondarily enter into the most varied connections with each other.

To consider every inborn mechanism an instinctual drive would be contrary to the concept of instinctual drive as it is commonly used in psychoanalysis and would presuppose the broader one (Eros-Thanatos) in which an instinctual drive is coordinated to every physiological process. Such a conception, however, would bypass rather than explain the special position of these apparatuses. Strictly speaking, there is no ego

[2] [Cf. "Psychiatrische Zwillingsprobleme." *Jahrbuch für Psychiatrie und Neurologie*, 50, 51, 1934.]

before the differentiation of ego and id, but there is no id either, since both are products of differentiation.[3] We may consider as inborn ego apparatuses those apparatuses which, after this differentiation, are unequivocally in the service of the ego. I want to stress again that once we assume inborn ego apparatuses, our view of purposiveness—which has always fluctuated—also changes: adaptation is only in part acquired anew by each generation, and is certainly not all wrung from the instinctual drives.[4]

The fact, which I have already stressed, that the newborn child has only a few functions at his disposal, will be advanced as an argument against these considerations. In answer I must point out that the *maturation processes* are not completed at the time of birth and there is growth in the sense of maturation outside of the mother's body also. This maturation, though we know little about it in many areas, must be recognized as an independent factor in addition to learning by experience, by memory, by exercise, by automatization, by identification, and by other mechanisms. Maturation and learning processes can be experimentally differentiated by means of the "co-twin-control method" introduced by Gesell and Thompson (1929): in one of two identical twins a performance is exercised, while in the other—the control—it is not; later on the control twin is subjected to the same learning process and the effect of maturation is inferred from the saving in learning. It might be useful to distinguish three kinds of developmental processes: those which occur without

[3] [This thought is more fully developed in "Comments on the Formation of Psychic Structure" (with Ernst Kris & Rudolph M. Loewenstein). *The Psychoanalytic Study of the Child*, 2:11-38. New York: International Universities Press, 1946.]

[4] [Cf. "The Mutual Influences in the Development of Ego and Id." *The Psychoanalytic Study of the Child*, 7:9-30. New York: International Universities Press, 1952.]

any essential and specific influence of the external world; those which are coordinated to typical experiences (that is, which are triggered by average expectable environmental situations, as already discussed); and finally, those which depend upon atypical experiences. The very course of maturation is in part a constitutional characteristic. This is a well-established fact for organic maturation. For example, the pathways between the paleoencephalon and neoencephalon do not yet function (are not yet myelinized) at the time of birth, nor is the maturation of motor pathways yet completed; the control of defecation presupposes maturation, and so on. We have always recognized the influence of maturation processes in the succession of the phases of libido organization also. Even the variation in the effect of experiences depends to some extent on the level of organization at which they are encountered, that is, upon maturation processes. We have already spoken of maturation processes, though we did not use the term, when discussing the heuristic possibilities and value of psychoanalysis in regard to the unfolding of constitutional givens. Considering the close relationship between the physiological and the mental, as we conceive of it, it is justified to assume mental maturation processes also, though it is less easy to think through the consequences of the assumption here than in the physiological realm. In many cases the ego functions no doubt depend directly on physiological maturation processes. However, to continue this line of thought would involve us in the psychophysical problem, and I would rather avoid that here.

We know that maturation processes are not entirely impervious to environmental influences. Yet they are independent factors which, both before and after birth, bring the inborn apparatuses successively into play, and determine at least grossly the rhythm of developmental processes. Thus not all improvements in adaptation result from experience.

EGO APPARATUSES. AUTONOMOUS EGO DEVELOPMENT

But we should note that the slow maturation of man is related to the prolongation of parental care; in this connection I remind you of Bolk's retardation principle. Typical differences in the rate of maturation of various functions lead, in man, to typical conflicts; for instance, the typical inability of the immature ego to provide gratification for drives is one of the reasons why instinctual drives are experienced as dangers (about other reasons, see below). Here the antithesis of maturation is learning (cf. Koffka, 1924), the paramount significance of which for man we have repeatedly stressed. It is not sufficient that the apparatuses have the potentiality for adapted function; their specific performances must be learned, that is, must be adapted. We are still unsure as to the role of conditioned reflexes in this process, but it is improbable that all the intelligence functions could be derived from them. (See Schilder [1935] and Kubie [1934] for the relationship between psychoanalysis and the theory of conditioned reflexes.) The *ability* to learn also seems to be partly determined by constitutional dispositions, which have been described as flexible in contrast to those dispositions which are not subject to alteration by learning.

Let us now return to the inherited ego apparatuses in particular and the inherited ego characteristics in general. Freud (1905b) suggested quite early that sexuality is inhibited not only by education but by certain inborn apparatuses: "But in reality this development [of sexual inhibitions] is organically determined, and fixed by heredity, and it can occasionally occur without any help at all from education" (pp. 177-178). Only recently has Freud given a somewhat more detailed discussion of inborn ego characteristics, assuming that the individual choice from among the possible defense mechanisms is determined by a constitutional factor: "It does not imply a mystical overvaluation of heredity if we think it credible that, even before the ego exists, its subsequent lines of development, tendencies and reactions are already determined" (1937, pp. 343-344).

Recent investigations make it fairly certain that the extent and direction even of intelligence (whose role in delaying motor discharge and in fulfilling a general inhibitory function we know) is at least partly determined by inherited dispositions. All the apparatuses mentioned here enter the service of the ego in the course of individual development. From this vantage point we can obtain a new outlook on the problem of the ego's primary antagonism toward the instinctual drive, which was raised by Anna Freud (1936). Since many of the ego apparatuses are inhibitory, and ego achievements are determined not only by mobile ego tendencies but also by ego apparatuses, it would follow that "the ego's distrust of the demands of instinctual drives" is the expression of a primary factor. (Another factor may be the already-mentioned partial antagonism between the survival of the individual and the survival of the species [the defenselessness of animals during copulation]. It seems obvious that the ego-psychological factor discussed above is of greater weight than this phylogenetic consideration.)

As we have just heard, Freud regarded the individual choice of defense mechanisms as in part constitutionally determined. We may also ask whether or not the defense processes are influenced by the maturation and exercise of the apparatuses of the conflict-free ego sphere. We have encountered this issue before, when, following Anna Freud, we traced the relation between defense and adaptation in normal development. It is possible that the developmental rhythm of these apparatuses is one of the determinants of the sequence in which defense methods arise. (The origin of these ego functions is a matter separate from the specific relationships to defense processes into which they enter.) The mechanisms of denial, avoidance, reaction formation, isolation, and undoing probably involve such determinants, but this is less likely in that other group of defenses which includes turning against the self, reversal into the opposite, etc. This view is consonant with Freud's conception that repression is a defense which presupposes the differentiation of the mental apparatus into ego and id.

Now it becomes clear why psychoanalytic ego psychology must come to grips with these problems. Our first considerations demonstrated that autonomous ego development is one of the prerequisites of all reality relations, and our further discussions made it probable that it is also the prerequisite for many other functions. Our arguments necessitated a detailed discussion of the ego apparatuses. In this connection, I stress again that no satisfactory definition of the concepts of ego strength and ego weakness is feasible without taking into account the nature and maturational stage of the ego apparatuses which underlie intelligence, will, and action.

Our contrast here of the ego and its apparatuses with the instinctual drives is in accord with (and supports in certain respects) the contrast of ego and instinctual drive current in psychoanalysis. I cannot discuss here the varied and interesting relations between instinctual drives and apparatuses, nor the relations between the cathectic conditions of the ego in general and those of the ego apparatuses. (Kardiner's [1932] interesting study provides some clues to the understanding of these problems.) The emphasis on the ego apparatuses may delineate more precisely our conception of the "self-preservative drives" which we have so far treated like a stepchild.

The psychology of the ego apparatuses seems to me a good example of the interlocking of conflict and adaptation (and achievement), and this brings us back to our starting point.

Many of these lengthy—but still incomplete—considerations are not psychoanalytic in a narrow sense, and some of them seem to have taken us quite far from the core of psychoanalysis. Much of our discussion has been in the nature of a program which must be filled in and made concrete by detailed empirical investigations. I will agree with you if you should find that I have been one-sided, stressing certain relationships and neglecting others of equal or greater importance—particularly those which usually concern us the most: that was my intention. I will be pleased if you should agree with me that the problems of autonomous ego development, of the structure and rank order of ego functions, of organization, of central regulation, of self-suspension of function, etc., and their relations to the concepts of adaptation and mental health, have a just claim on our attention.

Bibliography

ALEXANDER, F. (1921), Metapsychologische Betrachtungen. *Int. Z. Psa.,* 7:270-285.
—— (1924), A Metapsychological Description of the Process of Cure. *Int. J. Psa.,* 6:13-34, 1925.
—— (1933), The Relation of Structural and Instinctual Conflicts. *Psa. Quart.,* 2:181-207.
BALINT, M. (1937), Frühe Entwicklungsstadien des Ichs. Primäre Qbjektliebe. *Imago,* 23:270-288.
BALLY, G. (1933), Die frühkindliche Motorik im Vergleich mit der Motorik der Tiere. *Imago,* 19:339-366.
BERNFELD, S. (1930), *Trieb und Tradition im Jugendalter; kulturpsychologische Studien an Tagebüchern.* Leipzig: Barth, 1931.
—— (1931), Zur Sublimierungstheorie. *Imago,* 17:399-403.
—— (1937), Zur Revision der Bioanalyse. *Imago,* 23:197-236.
BIBRING, E. (1936), The Development and Problems of the Theory of the Instincts. *Int. J. Psa.,* 22:102-131, 1941.
BLEULER, E. (1920), Schizophrenie und psychologische Auffassung. Zugleich ein Beispiel, wie wir in psychologischen Dingen aneinander vorbeireden. *Allg. Z. Psychiat.,* 76:135-162.
BOLK, L. (1926), *Das Problem der Menschwerdung.* Jena: Fischer.
BORNSTEIN-WINDHOLZ, S. (1937), Missverständnisse in der psychoanalytischen Pädagogik. *Z. psa. Päd.,* 11:81-90.
BRIERLEY, M. (1936), Specific Determinants in Feminine Development. *Int. J. Psa.,* 17:163-180.
BÜHLER, C. (1928), *Kindheit und Jugend.* Leipzig: Hirzel.
BÜHLER, K. (1929), *Die Krise der Psychologie.* Jena: Fischer.
—— (1930), *The Mental Development of the Child.* New York: Harcourt.
CLAPARÈDE, E. (1924), Preface to J. Piaget, *The Language and Thought of the Child.* London: Routledge and Kegan Paul, 1948, pp. ix-xvii.

DELACROIX, H. (1936), La Croyance. La Psychologie de la Raison. *Nouveau Traité de Psychologie*, Vol. 5, Part 3. Paris: Alcan.

DEUTSCH, H. (1927), Über Zufriedenheit, Glück und Ekstase. *Int. Z. Psa.*, 13:410-419.

DEWEY, J. (1922), *Human Nature and Conduct; an Introduction to Social Psychology*. New York: Holt.

DRIESCH, H. (1908), *The Science and Philosophy of the Organism*. New York: Macmillan.

EHRENBERG, R. (1923), *Theoretische Biologie*. Berlin: Springer.

FENICHEL, O. (1928), Organ Libidinization Accompanying the Defense Against Drives. *The Collected Papers of Otto Fenichel*, 1:128-146. New York: Norton, 1953.

—— (1937a), The Concept of Trauma in Contemporary Psychoanalytical Theory. *The Collected Papers of Otto Fenichel*, 2:49-69. New York: Norton, 1954.

—— (1937b), Early Stages of Ego Development. *The Collected Papers of Otto Fenichel*, 2:25-48. New York: Norton, 1954.

FERENCZI, S. (1924), *Thalassa: A Theory of Genitality*. New York: Psychoanalytic Quarterly, Inc., 1938.

—— (1926), The Problem of the Acceptance of Unpleasant Ideas: Advances in Knowledge of the Sense of Reality. *Further Contributions to the Theory and Technique of Psycho-Analysis*. London: Hogarth Press, 1926, pp. 366-383.

FRENCH, T. M. (1937), Reality and the Unconscious. *Psa. Quart.*, 6:23-61.

FREUD, A. (1936), *The Ego and the Mechanisms of Defence*. New York: International Universities Press, 1946.

—— (1937), A Review of Psychoanalytic Pedagogy. Paper read at the Second Four-Countries Conference, Budapest, May 15-17, 1937.

FREUD, S. (1905a), Wit and Its Relation to the Unconscious. *The Basic Writings*. New York: Modern Library, 1938, pp. 631-803.

—— (1905b), Three Essays on the Theory of Sexuality. *Standard Edition*, 7:125-243. London: Hogarth Press, 1953.

—— (1911), Formulations Regarding the Two Principles in Mental Functioning. *Collected Papers*, 4:13-21. London: Hogarth Press, 1925.

—— (1915a), Instincts and Their Vicissitudes. *Collected Papers*, 4:60-83. London: Hogarth Press, 1925.

—— (1915b), The Unconscious. *Collected Papers*, 4:98-136. London: Hogarth Press, 1925.

—— (1917), *A General Introduction to Psycho-Analysis*. New York: Perma Giants, 1949.

—— (1920), Beyond the Pleasure Principle. *Standard Edition*, 18:3-64. London: Hogarth Press, 1955.

BIBLIOGRAPHY

—— (1921), *Group Psychology and the Analysis of the Ego.* London: Hogarth Press, 1948.
—— (1924a), Neurosis and Psychosis. *Collected Papers,* 2:250-254. London: Hogarth Press, 1924.
—— (1924b), The Passing of the Oedipus Complex. *Collected Papers,* 2:269-276. London: Hogarth Press, 1924.
—— (1925), Negation. *Collected Papers,* 5:181-185. London: Hogarth Press, 1950.
—— (1926a), An Romain Rolland. *Gesammelte Werke,* 14:553. London: Imago, 1948.
—— (1926b), *Inhibitions, Symptoms and Anxiety.* London: Hogarth Press, 1936.
—— (1927), *The Future of an Illusion.* New York: Liveright, 1949.
—— (1930), *Civilization and Its Discontents.* London: Hogarth Press.
—— (1931), Libidinal Types. *Collected Papers,* 5:247-251. London: Hogarth Press, 1950.
—— (1932), *New Introductory Lectures on Psychoanalysis.* New York: Norton, 1933.
—— (1937), Analysis Terminable and Interminable. *Collected Papers,* 5:316-357. London: Hogarth Press, 1950.
GESELL, A. & THOMPSON, H. (1929), Learning and Growth in Identical Infant Twins: An Experimental Study by the Method of Co-twin Control. *Genet. Psychol. Monogr.,* 6 (No. 1).
GOLDSTEIN, K. (1939), *The Organism.* New York: American Book Co.
GROOS, K. (1903), *Seelenleben des Kindes.* Berlin: Reuther & Reichard.
HARTMANN, H. (1927), *Die Grundlagen der Psychoanalyse.* Leipzig: Thieme.
—— (1928), Psychoanalyse und Wertproblem, *Imago,* 14:421-440.
—— (1933), Psychoanalyse und Weltanschauung. *Psa. Bewegung,* 5:416-429.
—— (1939), Psychoanalysis and the Concept of Health. *Int. J. Psa.,* 20:308-321.
HENDRICK, I. (1936), Ego Development and Certain Character Problems. *Psa. Quart.,* 5:320-346.
HERMANN, I. (1920), Intelligenz und tiefer Gedanke. *Int. Z. Psa.,* 6:193-201.
—— (1922), Randbemerkung zum Wiederholungszwang. *Int. Z. Psa.,* 8:1-13.
—— (1923), Organlibido und Begabung. *Int. Z. Psa.,* 9:297-310.
—— (1933), Zum Triebleben der Primaten. Bemerkungen zu S. Zuckerman: Social Life of Monkeys and Apes. *Imago,* 19:113-125.
JAENSCH, E. (1923), *Eidetic Imagery.* New York: Harcourt, Brace, 1930.
JANET, P. (1930), *L'Automatisme psychologique.* Paris: Alcan.

JONES, E. (1936), Psychoanalysis and the Instincts. *Papers on Psycho-Analysis.* Baltimore: Williams & Wilkins, 5th ed., 1948, pp. 153-169.
JUNG, C. G. (1920), *Psychological Types.* New York: Harcourt, Brace, 1923.
KARDINER, A. (1932), The Bio-Analysis of the Epileptic Reaction. *Psa. Quart.,* 1:375-483.
KLAGES, L. (1929), *Der Geist als Widersacher der Seele.* Leipzig: Barth.
KOFFKA, K. (1924), *The Growth of the Mind.* New York: Harcourt, Brace.
KRETSCHMER, E. (1921), *Physique and Character.* London: Kegan Paul, 1925.
—— (1922), *Medizinische Psychologie.* Leipzig: Thieme.
KRIS, E. (1934), The Psychology of Caricature. *Psychoanalytic Explorations in Art.* New York: International Universities Press, 1952, pp. 173-188.
—— (1939), On Inspiration. *Psychoanalytic Explorations in Art.* New York: International Universities Press, 1952, pp. 291-302.
KUBIE, L. S. (1934), Relation of the Conditioned Reflex to Psychoanalytic Technique. *Arch. Neurol. Psychiat.,* 32:430-435.
LAFORGUE, R. (1937), *The Relativity of Reality; Reflections on the Limitations of Thought and the Genesis of the Need of Causality.* New York: Nervous and Mental Disease Monographs, No. 66, 1940.
LANDAUER, K. (1927), Automatismen, Zwangsneurose und Paranoia. *Int. Z. Psa.,* 13:10-19.
LEUBA, J. (1937), In: R. A. Spitz, Familienneurose und neurotische Familie. Bericht über den IX. Kongress der Psychoanalytiker französischer Sprache 1936, in Nyon. *Int. Z. Psa.,* 23:548-560.
LÖWY, M. (1928), Versuch einer motorischen Psychologie mit Ausblicken auf die Charakterologie. *Jahrb. für Charakterologie,* 5:335-374.
MCDOUGALL, W. (1933), *The Energies of Men; A Study of the Fundamentals of Dynamic Psychology.* New York: Scribner.
MANNHEIM, K. (1935), *Man and Society in an Age of Reconstruction.* New York: Harcourt, Brace, 1940.
MUSIL, R. (1930, 1932), *A Man Without Qualities,* Vols. 1 and 2. London: Secker and Warburg, 1953, 1954.
NUNBERG, H. (1930), The Synthetic Function of the Ego. *Practice and Theory of Psychoanalysis.* New York: International Universities Press, 1955, pp. 120-136.
—— (1932), *Principles of Psychoanalysis.* New York: International Universities Press, 1955.
—— (1937), Theory of the Therapeutic Results of Psychoanalysis. *Practice and Theory of Psychoanalysis.* New York: International Universities Press, 1955, pp. 165-173.

BIBLIOGRAPHY

PARR, A. E. (1926), *Adaptiogenese und Phylogenese.* Berlin: Springer.

RADO, S. (1925), The Psychic Effects of Intoxicants: An Attempt to Evolve a Psycho-analytical Theory of Morbid Cravings. *Int. J. Psa.,* 7:396-413, 1926.

—— (1931), Ego Analysis and the Primacy of the Reality Principle. Lecture given at a special meeting of the Vienna Psychoanalytic Society, March, 1931.

REICH, W. (1933), *Charakteranalyse.* Vienna: Selbstverlag des Verfassers.

SCHELER, M. F. (1927), *Der Formalismus in der Ethik und die materiale Wertethik.* Bern: Francke, 1954.

SCHILDER, P. (1924), *Medical Psychology,* tr. David Rapaport. New York: International Universities Press, 1953.

—— (1928), *Gedanken zur Naturphilosophie.* Vienna: Springer.

—— (1933), Psychoanalyse und Biologie. *Imago,* 19:168-197.

—— (1935), Psychoanalyse und bedingte Reflexe. *Imago,* 21:50-66.

—— (1937), Zur Psychoanalyse der Benzhedrinwirkung. *Int. Z. Psa.,* 23:536-539.

SCHMIDEBERG, M. (1937), On Motoring and Walking. *Int. J. Psa.,* 18:42-53.

SHARPE, E. F. (1935), Similar and Divergent Unconscious Determinants Underlying the Sublimations of Pure Art and Pure Science. *Collected Papers on Psycho-Analysis.* London: Hogarth Press, 1950, pp. 137-154.

SIMMEL, G. (1922), *Zur Philosophie der Kunst.* Potsdam: Kiepenheuer.

SPITZ, R. A. (1936), The Differentiation and Integration of Psychic Processes. Lecture at the Vienna Psycho-analytical Society, May 20, 1936.

—— (1937), Wiederholung, Rhythmus und Langeweile. *Imago,* 23:171-196.

STÄRCKE, A. (1935), Die Rolle der analen und oralen Quantitäten im Verfolgungswahn und in analogen Systemgedanken. *Int. Z. Psa.,* 21:5-22.

STERN, W. (1914), *Psychology of Early Childhood up to the Sixth Year of Age.* New York: Holt, 1930, 6th ed.

TAUSK, V. (1913), Compensation as a Means of Discounting the Motive of Repression. *Int. J. Psa.,* 5:130-140, 1924.

UEXKÜLL, J. VON (1920), *Theoretical Biology.* New York: Harcourt, Brace, 1926.

VARENDONCK, J. (1921), *The Psychology of Daydreams.* New York: Macmillan.

WAELDER, R. (1932), The Psychoanalytic Theory of Play. *Psa. Quart.,* 2:208-224.

—— (1934a), Ätiologie und Verlauf der Massenpsychosen. Mit einem soziologischen Anhang: Über die geschichtliche Situation der Gegenwart. *Imago,* 21:67-91, 1935.

—— (1934b), The Problem of Freedom in Psycho-analysis and the Problem of Reality-testing. *Int. J. Psa.,* 17:89-108; 1936.

—— (1936a), Die Bedeutung des Werkes Sigm. Freuds für die Social- und Rechtswissenschaften. *Rev. Int. Théorie du droit,* 19:83-99.

—— (1936b), The Principle of Multiple Function: Observations on Over-determination. *Psa. Quart.,* 5:45-62.

WEBER, M. (1921), *The Theory of Social and Economic Organization.* New York: Oxford University Press, 1947.

WEISS, E. (1937), Psychic Defence and the Technique of Its Analysis. *Int. J. Psa.,* 23:69-80, 1942.

WERNER, H. (1929), *Comparative Psychology of Mental Development.* New York: International Universities Press, 1957, 3rd ed.

Name Index

Adler, A., 5
Alexander, F., 39, 91, 95, 109

Balint, M., 52, 109
Bally, G., 29, 50, 109
Becher, E., 29
Bernfeld, S., 30, 31, 45, 89, 109
Bibring, E., 8, 34, 38, 97, 101, 109
Bleuler, E., 100, 109
Bolk, L., 29, 33, 105, 109
Bornstein-Windholz, S., 75, 109
Brierley, M., 50, 109
Brill, A. A., 89
Bühler, C. H., 52, 97, 109
Bühler, K., 58, 61, 97, 109

Claparède, E., 61, 109

Delacroix, H., 60, 110
Deutsch, H., 53, 110
Dewey, J., 76, 88, 110
Dilthey, W., 64
Driesch, H., 30, 110

Ehrenberg, R., 38, 110

Federn, P., 7, 74
Fenichel, O., 6, 51, 52, 90, 94, 110
Ferenczi, S., 41, 42, 43, 45, 110
French, T. M., 42, 43, 98, 110
Freud, A., 4, 10, 12, 13, 14, 15, 16, 17, 19, 28, 29, 51, 58, 106, 110

Freud, S., 4, 6, 18, 20, 23, 25, 26, 28, 30, 32, 33, 34, 35, 38, 39, 41, 42, 45, 46, 48, 50, 52, 54, 57, 58, 59, 66, 71, 72, 75, 76, 77, 78, 82, 86, 89, 90, 95, 96, 97, 98, 99, 101, 105, 106, 110-111

Gesell, A., 103, 111
Goethe, J. W., 54
Goldstein, K., 93, 111
Groos, K., 88, 111
Guernsey, M., 97

Hartmann, H., 26, 31, 38, 40, 41, 48, 50, 55, 63, 64, 65, 74, 80, 87, 95, 97, 101, 102, 103, 111
Hendrick, I., 16, 111
Hermann, I., 10, 28, 60, 98, 111

Jaensch, E., 17, 111
Janet, P., 89, 111
Jaspers, K., 64
Jones, E., 9S, 112
Jung, C. G., 27, 112

Kardiner, A., 107, 112
Klages, L., 65, 112
Koffka, K., 105, 112
Kretschner, E., 27, 88, 112
Kris, E., 18, 37, 48, 77, 78, 103, 112
Kubie, L. S., 105, 112

NAME INDEX

Laforgue, R., 30, 66, 68, 112
Landauer, K., 90, 112
Leuba, J., 79, 112
Loewenstein, R. M., 48, 103
Löwy, M., 50, 112
Luther, M., 94

McDougall, W., 61, 112
Mannheim, K., 70, 73, 112
Musil, R., 69, 112

Nunberg, H., 40, 42, 52, 53, 63, 96, 97, 98, 101, 112

Parr, A. E., 20, 24, 27, 40, 113

Rado, S., 44, 52, 53, 113
Reich, W., 90, 113

Scheler, M. F., 47, 113
Schilder, P., 23, 59, 87, 100, 101, 105, 113

Schmideberg, M., 11, 13
Seneca, L., 84
Sharpe, E. F., 53, 113
Simmel, G., 62, 113
Spitz, R. A., 54, 96, 97, 98, 113
Spranger E., 64
Stärcke, A., 62, 113
Stern, W., 58, 60, 113

Tausk, V., 46, 113
Thompson, H., 103, 111

Uexküll, von, J., 24, 27, 41, 48, 113

Varendonck, J., 18, 113

Waelder, R., 20 33, 55, 71, 93, 97, 113-114
Weber, M., 67, 75, 114
Weiss, E., 55, 114
Werner, H., 53, 114

Subject Index

Action, 86ff., 100ff.
   affective (irrational), 20, 67-70, 72-73, 92
   rational, 20, 36, 57ff., 65, 67-68, 70-73, 75-76, 86, 92
   realism of, 86-87
Adaptation, 22ff., 38ff., 48ff.
   alloplastic, 19, 20, 24, 26-27, 31, 71
   and automatization, 91ff.
   and biology, 6, 28
   and conflict, 8, 39-40, 107
   and conflict-free sphere, 10, 11, 24-25
   and detour, 18-19
   and education, 12-13, 31, 82
   and ego regulation, 25
   and fitting together, 40, 64-65
   and instinctual drives, 27, 28, 46, 57-58
   and intelligence (knowledge), 19, 60-61, 66, 68-69; see also *Action*
   and society, 29-32, 54, 75-76, 103
   and success (adjustment), 3, 23, 32, 36
   and superego, 30, 52
   and thinking, 62; see also *Intelligence*
   autoplastic, 19, 20, 24, 27, 78
   by choice of environment, 19-20, 26-27, 31-32
   by learning, 24, 49
   defense as; see *Defenses*
   disturbance of, 40, 54-55, 62
   ego as organ of; see *Ego*
   guarantees of, 14, 17, 25, 45-46, 52; see also *Apparatuses*
   in biology, 23-24, 54
   of individual and species, 27-28, 66
   passive and active, 32
   regressive, 36, 53-58, 77
   see also *Pleasure principle; Reality principle*
Adaptedness
   means of, 24; see also *Apparatuses, primary*
   state of, 23-24, 49, 92
Anticipation, 43, 68, 70
Apparatuses (autonomous), 11, 15, 16, 17, 25, 29, 46-47, 49, 87-88, 90, 91, 100ff., 105-106, 107
   and development, 15, 25, 43, 46-47, 50, 104-105, 107
   and drive, 15, 26, 29, 100-103
   as adaptation guarantees, 17, 45-46
   occasional, 100
   primary, 11, 14, 15, 49, 50, 100ff., 105
   primary disorders of, 40
   relationship to defenses, 9, 10, 14, 15, 16, 17, 106

SUBJECT INDEX

Apparatuses (autonomous) (cont'd)
  secondary, 25-26, 88ff.; see also
    Change of function
  undifferentiated phase and, 49, 102-103
  see also *Motility; Memory; Perception*
Art, 37, 77-78
Automatization, 87ff., 95-96; see also *Automatisms; Change of function; Formular abbreviation*
Automatisms, 26, 86ff., 94, 97-99
  and adaptation, 91-92
  and the preconscious, 89-90
  and the repetition compulsion, 95ff.
  vs. flexibility, 92, 95
  see also *Automatization; Change of function; Repetition compulsion*
Biology, 23
  and psychoanalysis, 6, 23, 32-35
  see also *Phylogenesis; Psychoanalysis, biological character of*
Change of function, 25-26, 49-50, 77
Conflict, 7, 8-9, 10, 13, 15, 21, 38, 107
  and ego development, 7-8, 11, 13
  average expectable, 11-12, 54-55, 105
  pathological and normal, 12, 80ff.
Conflict-free ego sphere, 3ff., 8, 9, 10, 20, 38, 55, 81, 100
  and adaptation, 10, 22
  and conflict, 8-9, 16
  and defense, 9, 10, 15, 16
  and education, 12ff., 82ff.

and psychoanalytic therapy, 7, 9, 12, 26, 55, 81, 90-91, 94
regulations of, 75
see also *Development; Apparatuses*
Defenses, 9, 10, 12, 14, 47, 51, 63, 90, 106
  and adaptation, 9, 14, 15 16, 26, 40, 51, 81
  and synthetic function, 51
  and thinking, 63
  choice of, 9, 10, 14, 105, 106
  precursors of; see under the immediately following two headings
  relationship to ego apparatuses, 9, 10, 14, 15, 16, 17, 106
  relationship to instinctual drives, 49, 102, 107
  see also *Conflict-free ego sphere*
Delay, 59, 62, 106
Detour, 18, 19, 36, 58, 77
Development, 8, 9, 11, 34, 46, 48ff., 100ff., 103-105
  and conflict, 11-12, 13, 16
  biological and social factors in, 32-34, 84-85
  conflict-free, 8, 10-12, 15, 41, 100ff.
  of relation to environment, 51-52
  see also *Ego, development*
Differentiation, 49-50, 52-54, 55-56, 60, 69,
  precocity of, 53
  see also *Ego, differentiation from id*
Direct observation, 8, 10, 12, 52

Education, 3, 12-13, 31, 80ff., 84-85
Ego
  and automatisms, 88ff., 92-95

[118]

SUBJECT INDEX

and defenses, 10
apparatuses; see *Apparatuses*
as organ of adaptation, 27, 36-37, 50-51
as organ of equilibrium, 39; see also *Equilibrium*
autonomy, 12, 26, 41, 50, 101, 107, 108; see also *Apparatuses (autonomous), primary; Apparatuses (autonomous), secondary*
constitutional factors in, 50, 101-102; see also *Apparatuses*
development, 8, 10-12, 15, 22, 41, 43, 48ff., 53, 100ff., 104-105
and conflict, 8-9, 10-11, 13, 15-16
autonomous, 12, 41, 101, 107, 108
differention from id, 48, 49-50, 52, 102-103, 107
functions, 7, 8-9, 10-11, 12, 14-15, 20, 22, 43, 46, 47, 53-54, 55, 62, 78, 92, 94-95, 101, 102, 105, 106-107
integrative, 74ff.; see also *Synthetic function*
and pleasure, 43, 46, 97; see also *Pleasure in functioning*
rank order of, 55, 92-93, 95
interests, 10, 67, 70, 74
mobility of, 78, 88, 92, 94-95
partial concepts, 95
psychology, 4, 6-7, 8, 10, 13
regression in the service of; see *Regression*
regulations, 25, 49-50, 57-58, 72, 74ff., 95, 98
relation to reality of, 17, 30-32, 45, 51; see also *Environment*
strength, 15-16, 56, 107
vs. instinctual drive, 28, 106

see also *Apparatuses (autonomous); Synthetic function; Adaptation*
Environment, 7, 17, 23-24, 29-30, 33-34, 35, 45, 48
average expectable, 23, 35, 46, 51, 55, 76, 104
choice of; see *Adaptation*
conflict with, 11
dependence of organism on, 28-29, 40-41, 45, 55, 58, 74, 91-92
independence of organism (and/or ego) from, 40, 58, 59, 60, 78, 102
mastery of, 18-19, 21, 39, 45, 50, 58, 60, 70
see also *Reality; Adaptation*
Equilibrium, 23, 31, 38-39, 70
External reality; external world; see *Environment*

Fantasy, 16-19, 36, 42, 77
biological significance of, 18
Fitting in, 24
"Fitting together," 36, 38ff., 53, 55, 65, 66
and synthetic function, 40
Formular abbreviation, 88, 95

Goals, 26, 68, 70-71, 75-76, 82-83
rational, 67, 75
therapeutic, 27

Habit, 61, 68, 88-89, 91

Inner world, 53, 57, 58
Instinct, 48
and instinctual drives, 29, 48-49
and intelligence, 61ff.
equipment of man, 29, 49
Instinctual drive, 34, 43, 44, 45-46, 57-58
and adaptation, 27, 28, 46, 57-58

SUBJECT INDEX

Instinctual drive (cont'd)
  and development, 13-14, 46, 104
  constitution, 29, 50
  external world vs., 29-30
Integration; see *Synthetic function*
Intelligence, 16, 17, 60ff., 65, 69-73, 106
  and adaptation, 19, 60-61, 65ff., 68-69, 73
  and defense, 14
  and value, 83-84
  biological function of, 60-61, 68
  organizing role of, 69ff., 73, 92
  primacy of regulation by, 56, 71-72
Internalization, 40, 57ff.
Interpretation (psychoanalytic), 63-64

Learning, 8, 11, 14, 18, 27, 29, 47, 49, 95, 98, 103, 105

Man
  relation to environment of, 30-32, 51; see also *Environment*
  slow maturation of, 28-29, 105
  vs. animal, 20, 26-27, 28, 48-49, 58
Maturation; see *Development*
Means-ends relations, 26, 60, 67, 94
Memory, 8, 15, 59
Mental health, 12, 18, 23, 32, 35, 55, 69, 80ff., 93-95; see also *Conflict, average expectable*
Methodology, 4-5, 34-35, 45, 52
Motility, 8, 11, 16, 50, 59-60, 87-88, 90, 101 102

Organization 40, 47, 69, 71, 73

Perception, 17, 58-59, 60, 101, 102
Phylogenesis, 24, 28, 40, 45-46, 49, 61

Pleasure in functioning, 46, 97
Pleasure principle, 39, 41ff., 86, 95-96, 98
Psychoanalysis
  and conscious qualities, 6, 59
  and other psychologies, 4-6, 9-10, 17, 19, 23
  and sociology, 20-21
  as a development of thought, 64-65, 70, 71
  as therapy, 7, 55, 71, 72, 81, 83, 90-91
  biological character of, 5, 23, 28, 31, 32-33, 34, 44
  objectives of, 4-5, 9
  see also *Interpretation*

Rank order, biological, 13, 40-41, 44, 55, 93; see also *Ego functions, rank order of*
Reality
  as ally against drives, 29-30
  denial of by fantasy, 16, 17
  internal, 19
  knowledge of, 19, 66; see also *Adaptation; Intelligence*
  principle, 38ff., 41ff., 86
  the broader, 44
  -syntonic, 3, 66, 87
  testing, 18, 41, 53, 60, 62
  biological significance of, 17-18
  see also *Environment; Adaptation*
Reconstruction (psychoanalytic), 52, 63-64
Regression, 36, 50
  in the service of the ego, 37, 58, 94, 95
Regulation
  by the external world, 41, 45, 55, 74, 92, 98

SUBJECT INDEX

principles, 39, 40, 41, 43-44, 46, 49, 74ff., 98, 101-102
rational and irrational 36, 55, 72-73, 92-93
see also *Ego regulations; Environment; Reality; Inner world*
Religion, 18, 78-79, 82
Repetition compulsion, 39, 41, 42-43, 95-99
and automatism, 90, 95ff.
and pleasure principle, 95ff., 98

Survival, 24, 38, 107
and pleasure principle, 41, 44
Social compliance, 31-32
Society, 21, 76
and adaptation, 27-28, 30-32
biological function of, 29, 30-31, 32-33
Sociology, 12, 20-21, 32-33
Stimulus barrier, 57, 91
Structure, 26
development, 52

Superego, 11, 15, 30, 40, 52, 59, 62, 67, 75
Synthetic function, 18, 37, 40, 47, 51-56, 63, 69, 74ff.
and equilibrium, 39
biological significance of, 55

Talents, 10, 15, 17
Thinking, 8, 14, 17, 34, 40, 53, 57ff., 59-60, 63, 74-75
adaptive function of, 62
and reality, 14, 60
biological function of, 34, 58-59, 61, 65-66
in the psychoanalytic situation, 62ff.
scientific, 18, 37, 59, 64, 72
see also *Fantasy*
Twins, 102-103

Value, 67, 75ff., 82ff.
and adaptation, 75
-rational action, 67, 75-76
Will, 74-75, 93